A LUCENT FIRE

A LUCENT FIRE

NEW AND SELECTED POEMS BY
PATRICIA SPEARS JONES

INTRODUCTION BY MARY BAINE CAMPBELL

WHITE PINE PRESS ❋ BUFFALO, NEW YORK

White Pine Press
P.O. Box 236
Buffalo, New York 14201
www.whitepine.org

Copyright © copyright 2015 by Patricia Spears Jones

Introduction © copyright 2015 by Mary Baine Campbell

All rights reserved. This work, or portions thereof, may not be reproduced in any form without the written permission of the publisher.

Acknowledgments continue on page 201, which constitutes an extension of this copyright page.

"The Birth of Rhythm and Blues," "In Like Paradise/Out Like the Blues," "Encounter and Farewell," "If I Were Rita Hayworth," "The Usual Suspect," "San Francisco, Spring 1986," "Baby Hair Shirt," "Glad All Over," "The Perfect Lipstick," "Sly & the Family Stone Under the Big Tit/Atlanta, 1973," "5:25 A.M.," "Thief's Song," "Measure," "What the God of Fire Charged Me," and "New Blues" reprinted with permission from *The Weather That Kills* (Coffee House Press, 1995). Copyright © 1995 Patricia Spears Jones.

Publication of this book was made possible, in part, by grants from the National Endowment for the Arts, which believes that a great nation deserves great art; and with public funds from the New York State Council on the Arts, a State Agency.

ART WORKS.
arts.gov

State of the Arts

NYSCA

Cover art: *Untitled* by Sandra Payne. Used by permission of the artist.
Author photo by Rachel Eliza Griffiths

First Edition

ISBN: 978-1-935210-69-6

Printed and bound in the United States of America.

Library of Congress Control Number: 2014960010

There are many people to whom this collection is commended, but none more than my mother, Lillie B. Dodd Spears Jones (1919–2013). She was a woman of great curiosity and spirituality, serious style—you do not have to be rich to have it—and deep commitment to her family, to education, to music, poetry, to healing (she was a nurse), and to community, a true race woman. She gave me, my brother William and my sister Gwendolyn much love and nurture and a model to follow as best we can. I would not be a poet if not for her. "This little light of mine"

celebrate the feasts of my testament

for here fire scatters its robes

extending its steps through the joy of questions

> "The Bard's *Mawwal*" from *Quartet of Joy* by Muhammad Afifi Matar translated by Ferial Ghazoul & John Verlenden

Contents

Introduction

There is a world in this book.

It bears a strange resemblance to the real one, except that it is beautiful, strained and filtered through a human heart. Then cooked in the lucent fire of Patricia Jones' poetic oven.

(Not every oven cooks with lucent fire.)

This world has a geography. Patricia Spears Jones has been turning New York and Boston and Arkansas and Atlanta and San Francisco and Paris and Amsterdam and Germany and Cuba and ancient China, the Atlantic Ocean, the canyons and mountains of the West, the streets and parks of Brooklyn into poems for half my life, as a poet and critic and commentator on the arts scene in many cities—above all that great Babylon of the arts and humans, Gotham City. Where she lives, knowing everyone, performing everywhere, catching every show, blogging before there were blogs, rooting for every young writer and artist coming up, teaching the newcomers how to open their minds and hearts while holding a pen, at the same time pouring tea for the Ladies to bring in the New Year and celebrating their achievements, writing till the wee hours . . . as her tired "Office Worker" says, in a projective fantasia on an alternative Plath: "Revise that poem from two weeks ago / lights out at 2 A.M."

So a force, whatever her losses in this dark world, of joy, if that is what art is: a force of joy. But I am writing in the shadow of the massacre yesterday in Charleston, the cold-blooded, explicitly racist murder of nine members of a prayer group in Mother Emanuel A. M. E. Church, the oldest A. M. E. church in the South—burned to the ground after a slave rebellion in 1821, outlawed in 1834, destroyed anew by an earthquake in 1886, now drenched in the blood of its own pastor and congregants. It is impossible not to feel tonight, as I read these poems, the fragility of the world they so lovingly invoke and celebrate and mourn.

But Patricia Spears Jones would have none of my fatalism tonight, knowing the story of that church's many resurrections, knowing the strength of poetry to survive the worst we can do to each other, and running up the mast as she does, in spite of everything, the brave top-gallant of delight.

The aesthetics of this collection of collections, spanning decades but adhering always to the same key values, born from the same sense of what poetry is for, are capacious. You can spot one of her poems from a mile away: they are poems of wide and deep appreciation for the boundless myriad of beings, things, creatures, moments, languages, voices—that is one of the most important ways they feed me. Many of these poems, or the moments of high color in them, bring to our attention the quotidian splendors of a world within our grasp and view: "the teasing power of Big Boy Crudup or Ruth Brown's / haughty insinuations or the crazy men in Macon with their too tight / suits pants and dicks as long as legend permits," the "moment in *Jack Smith* where Smith pushes back the elaborate / fake Arab headgear, mascara smearing so slowly that decade fades away," "the brothers in huge Afros, / amulets and attitudes stalk the round of the Big Tit" (but the amulets take us to Egypt, to the magicians of the Maghreb), "Darjeeling tea in a generous cup" (we feel the distance of Darjeeling, the excitement of drinking leaves brought so far to us), "language as liquid as Portuguese, as supple as English" (how lovely to hear our language praised, in words whose assonance links them to the liquid of exotic Portuguese!), "the stone coyotes that guard the Inari Shrine" (in Prospect Park's Botanic Garden). The romance and glamor of it all! Yet none of the poems I just quoted leave Brooklyn, except the one that goes to Georgia.

Quotidian splendors aren't all though, not by a long shot. This is poetry that analyzes our culture as well as offering up its beauties, pleasures, crimes. We stand in need of analysis and these poems do not shirk the task. Tonight the grim-faced, tired president didn't know what to say: he admitted, with Jon Stewart, that the violence and hatred were going to go on and that he could do nothing to make it stop. I sometimes wonder what would happen if politicians read poetry every day. Patricia Jones was always trying to tell you: "I . . . know why I have always respected aging Black men. / To have defied the bullets ever ready to find their targets, / these are men of immeasurable *luck*." "In what cinema are the dreams of mass destruction / so dear as ours?" On running into a glass wall at a job interview: "If you're lucky, you don't fall / If you're lucky, you don't see stars / If you're lucky, you stand there / If you're lucky, you don't bleed / If you're lucky, the nice white guy asks / 'Are you alright?' / If you're lucky, the nice black guy asks / 'Are you alright?' and he adds 'I've done that twice.'" "De Man, De Woman, Dis Soulless Nation with the odd / White Man in charge—on a ranch, a barge, fishing—whatever? // Violent death follows. / Best to join the Ambassador of Soul, who brought / us the ache and art of Black America, claiming // Patriarchy of funk and feeling just about as good as you can get."

I remember being warned in a college poetry workshop, "Never write poems about poetry," and a colleague where I teach once forbade his students to write poems about photographs or paintings ("too easy"). Both might have made room for Auden's "Musée des Beaux Arts" or Yeats' "Adam's Curse" or the ekphrasis of Homer and Virgil. I hope they would make room for Patricia Spears Jones as well, as one of the gifts of this opus is her refusal to keep the art and theater and music and textile and sewing and above all poetry that fuel and focus her life—and if you think for a minute, all of our lives—out of the world of her own poetry. In this again Jones' world resembles the real world, that place of intersection of all our lives and visions and creations (and alas, un-creations). And again, in line with the value of aliveness that orients this collection, from "Early" to "New and Uncollected," the arts make their appearance most often through the medium of artists, alive and in motion. The moving, singing, typing, painting, acting, street-walking, drinking, loving, shopping, thinking, shoe-wearing characters of *Lucent Fire* include Billie Holiday, Rita Hayworth, James Brown, Sly & the Family Stone, Sylvia Plath, Kara Walker, Lynda Hull, Marilyn Monroe, Thulani Davis, Mary J. Blige, Borges, George E. Hunt, Thomas Sayers Ellis, Etta James, Aretha Franklin, Kurt Cobain, Fellini, Fats Domino, Rodgers and Hammerstein (and Hart), Mabou Mines, the Wooster Group, Godard, Neruda, Mishima, Beuys, Lacan, Diamonda Galas, Akilah Oliver. . . .

This list reminds me of two artists not mentioned but inhabiting Jones' poetic world, two women forbears who provide affordances: Gwendolyn Brooks and Marilyn Hacker. Both are poets who render places (not regions or nations) with loving, clear-eyed—and -eared—attention, as does Jones; Hacker in particular renders individual people too—writers above all (who haunt Brooks' more modernist early poetry, but linguistically, not as characters). Brooks and Hacker surprised their early readers with their persistent, frame-breaking attention to specific place and person, to character, to narrative, phenomena understood in the wake of Modernism to belong to prose fiction, if anywhere, and in the polemical dawn of Postmodernism to belong (for some reason) to false consciousness. But when American poetry at large re-awoke to narrative in the 80s, it was often to a kind of hyper-personal narrative, hatched within a view of lyric poetry as essentially autobiographical. Brooks' third-person narrative lines had been fictional representations, and Jones' vignettes are often frankly fictional as well, even fantastical—as in her hybrid fantasies of Sylvia Plath, or of Borges building a library near a Norwegian fjord. Some of her narratives are clotheslines on which to hang a tableau, like a mountain hike with friends in Idaho in the signature poem, "What Beauty Does." Some are snippets of a day or night spent with others at work or play, or alone with the haunting absence of a lover or a dead friend: they are narrative in the sense that the people in them are in motion, moved by desires and fears, but they are not constructed to reach for a climax or end with a resolution. And they are no more "autobiographical" than the artistry of Brooks or Hacker. They scoop up and use everything in their path to make their world, and some of what is there is the poet's own experience: precious for what it says to all who have shared that experience, instructive to all who have not.

It is probably right, then, to call Patricia Spears Jones painterly, though her paintings sing and shout and make noise, the people in them move: they do not sit for their portraits. Like Hopper, whom she references, her paintings spotlight regular folks in their regular places—often in the past, sometimes in the present. It is getting harder to find regular folks or regular places in the urban consumerist dream of the twenty-first century but Jones manages the bling and violence of the present too right next to the elegiac poems that give us Aretha, Fats Domino, Plath and Borges, living and moving in their gone world.

For the world Patricia Jones gives us is full of ghosts (including Albert Ayler's in "Ghosts") and living people both, and of history as well as this hard present that can make it impossible to imagine writing a poem on another tired night. Because it includes death as well as life, including untimely death, violent death, mass death, deaths that represent scourges common to all Americans but that visit with particular ferocity the African Americans of this unfair, uncured country.

Not the right note to end on, even on this sobering, sad night. Patricia Spears Jones is a poet who faces all that there is to face (that's what I ask of any poet, but do not get from every poet). But she doesn't wallow in gloom or shriek with outrage. She tells stories and paints pictures and sings favorite lines from everyplace and everyone but especially from her America. The country out there beyond our personal memories and experiences, or hers, is in the dark days of its imperium, a country best seen from abroad or from the point of view of the structurally dispossessed, by artists who are not tempted beyond the strength of consciousness to benefit from its racism, its totalitarianism, its profiteering, its wars. "Heart's rage glistens, the roads are hazardous / but take them, we must." That Jones aspires to be an American poet, a Black poet, a woman poet, a citizen poet means she aspires to hope in spite of all of this: "I stand // in front of beautiful things and curb my appetite for murder." Her art is the ladder by which she climbs to hope (a place after all in her home state of Arkansas), bringing us along for the big view.

—Mary Baine Campbell

EARLY POEMS

Wearing My Red Silk Chinese Jacket

1.

Children of the Pentecost like moles
burrow through this city of shadows
fleeing light.

2.

There are dialectics when the spirit
calls forth the tongues on Sunday mornings.
There the Sisters converse with the blood
of all the saints.
There the Brothers shift their dignity
from one foot to the other before their bodies
forget the necessity of gravity.
There the smoke rises joyous as if
from the ashes of a terrible defeat.
There are no dialectics when the spirit
rips open the heart of the Children of Darkness
and takes them back through the sun to home.

3.

Ancestress in woodblock
Her babe torn from her side by slave traders
Their hats cocked sideways.
Their eyes rapacious.
Her lips large.
Her cry clear as the sky
Above the auction block
A universe composed of empty tears.
Ancestress in woodblock screaming
across the Middle Passage

quaking on this makeshift stage
What has Jesus done for you?

4.

Who owns the Sun?
A question for terrorists.
I got this ability to see three sides
of each issue and know that all of them
are wrong.
I sat on the Mourning Bench, but never cried.
Jesus did not want me.
Jesus did not comfort me.
Jesus took a walk across the street
went into a bar and ordered a double whiskey
Straight up.
Jesus hung with the tough guys till they bled
Him good and sealed him in some big tomb.
Known locally as the Sepulcher. It was the drunk tank.
His fast friends came and got him out of there.
But Jesus couldn't admit to liking moonshine
whiskey or the company of tattooed men.
What would the choir members think?

5.

There she sits in regal nudity.
No scepter, no sash.
Her brown skin bespeaks the earthen hues
of her voluptuous body. The face kneeling at
her crotch wants her. Wants to eat her. Wants
all of the earth within her. This face forgets
to leer. This is serious. You come to these
islands to escape civilization. What do you find:
Civilization? This ego cannot stand this confusion.
She is mine, ego dreams

She is mine.
I paint her naked because she needs only skin.
I paint her naked because she has beautiful breasts
& I want them to know where I've supped.
I paint her because I can't eat dirt and she is—as
The elements are—available.
Her smile is hers.
I take only the deliberate angles of her body
& dine.
Ancestress in woodblock
What has Jesus done for you?

6.

What bright women turned the spindles;
dyed the thread? Jungle colors. Who called
Bebop "Chinese music"? A Sunday in Chinatown
an old woman touched my jacket. Admiration.
She say to brown-skinned girl in red silk Chinese jacket
"good"
"good"
& walks off with her friend
into the metallic clatter of the traffic.
I stunned
cannot twist my mind from the heart
of gospel music—how it stirred the soul's ear
and crowded the mind's eye.
And when the bristling gestures of busy waiters
recall our mutual houses of contempt
I see the wonder in that woman's eye and know that
fleeing light is not always about escape.

7.

The hand that rocks
The body rolls

The good Lord comes down to earth, on occasion
& clasps a poor misguided man to his bosom
Makes him a minister and sets his mouth
Open with words that flow like a flood in late
Spring. His charm in his hip motion when he roars
across the pulpit like a linebacker stalking prey.
The backsliders signify.
The better, stronger get on up and shout!
Soaking in holy water—drums, guitars, the choir's
Rhapsodic singing and clapping
The whirling ceases
like the cry of the women and men
who separated across state lines still remembered
their family names.
Brother to Brother.
Sister to Sister.
Crying in the wilderness, blessed America.
Creeping through canyons constructed
on the principles of implosions.
Crafty, devilish, yes
You, in your bad madness
Not even hip to history or the possibility
of good news.
You there, torn up; tear it up!
Drugged, drummed down, daily eating
The crumbs from your mama's table
wearing the last dregs of an impossible
nightmare
Tell me
Tell me
What has Jesus done for you?

Spanish Lesson

La negra   term of endearment
El blanco   dream of riches
One woman   una mujer
One Man   un hombre

      Tongues that begin to taste alike
Tense geography
La bomba es la danza divine de los Africanos

White shoes ice the city dance floors sharp
That old pencil-thin moustache dream is dead
Because salsa *es caliente y suave* and the men
Want brass to blast away the crumbling buildings
The dope, the young dead carried away with candles
Glowing

Las chichas dulces trabajan the garment district
Cursing when necessary the others damned
In the push and pull

Forgive the old pirate his coffers of rum—the *Ingles*
Got more than they bargained for—the city pulsating
From borough to borough *con ritmos necesarios*

Las mujeres lindas bochinche on 14th Street
About the one with his tongue hanging out
While Héctor Lavoe lured the ladies
With a reel of promises made sweeter by his
Yo, no sé
Yo, no sé

Outlaw African breezes perfume the shining dance floors
Speaking a language never sanctioned in the New World
Libations poured from old pirate's stock

Please the ancestors Here in North America where
Carmen Miranda and her mulatto progeny sashayed they stuff
Across Hollywood camera eye
Like comets christening the tropics

¿Si, como no?

Mythologizing Always: Seven Sonnets

I.

Here is the place where declarations
are made/where the heart takes precedence
the gleam goes bland
This is the heart part/intense improvisation
on the I/THOU axis
pity the poor actors (darlings)dust
in their throats (choking) dialogue ancient
(concentrated chatter dictated by clouds)

click of whispers
dammed up phrases   {mythologizing always)
Moans move through their limbs like wind through
Trees talking mad talk 'cross the illuminated
Avenues of hard cities.

II.

Take the skin
Take off the skin
Remove the vital organs one by one
especially the heart
What is left
The skeleton
The skeleton is made of calcium
magnesium, phosphorous et cetera:
an amazing catalogue of chemicals
You are holding in your arms
an amazing catalogue of chemicals
The elements clash tenderly
Sparking compounds that move like eels
Under touch.

III.

Dime falls, your voice rises (fevered)
It's keen, the way the wind whips this
Garbage up and around like a father
Swinging his baby we are holding hands
And yes, giggling no force can stop us now
We are singing all the James Brown songs
We know helpless off-key, but exhilarated
Columbus Avenue breakdown: how the puddles
In the sidewalks radiate splendor/glass
Broken against high-rise buildings beckon
We are hungry the shifting children salsa
And you may be our feast, please linger
You offer me your laughter
I take the sweat from y our cheeks and hum.

IV.

Taste like tears—sea flaked and heated—
Taste like try again and get nowhere,
Maybe, this is the sonnet that mimes itself
Sequences silent and perceptive
The "might have saids"
The stomach-eating rage
The power of conversation is in its
Possibilities of Interpretation
(here's where the mime becomes important
because the words sound so dumb)
And here's where the anxiety dance gets choreographed.
It goes like this: You turn Clockwise.
I turn Counter-Clockwise. We stop, stumble
Resolve our steps. Begin again.

V.

You slipped into something dangerous
after attending to your intimate conferences
Thirsty friends forever requesting water
Or is it blood they want?　　　Your blood.
Somebody's screaming. Is it me?
Here on the side street being a sideshow
For passersby. You put on your silver armor.
I have only my quaint devotion.
It is not enough.　　　You say
I can't eat your food, baby, but I still like your cooking.
Did I trip?　　Did you?　That Mingus
record is still revolving. You smile
serenely.　　　I can barely breathe.

VI.

If I could waste myself, I'd do it here
In public. Curse your name till my tongue bled.
The same tongue that searched out the
darkest spot on your back and licked it like chocolate.
Curse your name like you were some
Broken god in need of further profaning.

But I am no good at playing: victim.
Sadness is so private. These tears on the
Uptown Express. Take that tired song off
the constant stereo. It keeps reminding me
That what brought me to you was music.
You said you never lied to me. Fucker.

You take the exit sign home with you.
But I won't become invisible.

Change in Seasons or The Break-up Sonnet VII

Feels like San Francisco /that chill
Sun burns it away fast and the cut
on your index finger is healed up now
Time does its duty by bodies and the weather

There are scars always
Faithful clicks on the psychic metronome
A shiver in the limbs perhaps
A grimace just before the smile

But holding on to the dead is worse
You move on /move away
Let your shoulders carve a space for some sky
And you don't ever, ever look back
For fear those Biblical tales are true
And you never could stand the taste of salt.

from THE WEATHER THAT KILLS

The Birth of Rhythm and Blues

From the Billie Holiday Chronicles

Mid-February in America. Cold everywhere but Florida,
parts of California, and New Orleans, where Mardi Gras ends
in a gale of coconuts, trinkets, streamers and libations.

My daddy come back from the war, tall, slender, handsome.
Lonely in Korea, lonely in Arkansas. Lonely enough
to court my mother. Tall, pretty and tired
of her drunken husband, their store going bankrupt
and the grimy reality of small town daily life. A small town is
gossip and errands, work and more work. Schools closed in
spring (chopping cotton) and early fall (picking cotton),
the death-defying lives of all Black people—high yaller to coal black.
A Black woman's life is like double jeopardy.
All you win are dreams for your children
and the right amount of lies to make waking worthwhile.
Call it sweet talk from a colored soldier back from the snows of
          Korea.
Back from the nasty jokes, the threats, the fights in This Man's Army.
Back to America. Still alive.

Mama is early in her thirties. Promised so little and then hungry
for the world. For a world larger than the screen door that slams
early morning, and the reeking breath of a man once handsome and
          friendly
and too easy with money. His money. Her time. He's beginning to
          die.
Liver rotting away. He passes blood and thinks of a knife fight,
some juke joint when a Louis Jordan song blasted off the
jukebox. So fast, that song.
And funny too. Everybody shaking. Pelvic shaking.
But then a man's mouth opened, then another, and then slash-high
cheekbones and graveyard eyes. Some niggers don't know when to
          shut up.

A red light bulb shivers like sunset before a harvest moon.
My mother's husband singes the pain with whiskey. It burns
the lining of his stomach. Starts the ulcer. Precipitates the cancer.
My mother's stomach grows and grows. New moon. New hope.

My mother sings her own songs. Humming songs.
Something low into the earth
where the hurting stops and healing begins.
That point where Billie hit
bottom and found the start of a global nightmare.
Every walking man wounded again and again. Pierced in eye,
belly, tongue, penis, anus, shoulder, foot.
All the walking men bleeding and bleeding into music's deep well.
Quenching her joy. Clotting her dreams.
Following her swaying hips screaming GIMME GIMME
GIMME
Billie's at the corner where the dope man slinks. Willow in a Harlem
        breeze.
She's strung out again. Big Irish cops, with nothing better to do,
        follow her.
She's feeling evil. Starts her humming. They want
to drink my Irish blood.
They want that back. She's laughing low.

In New Orleans, Professor Longhair has taken to the piano
and rumbled up a rhythm as steady as Saturday night loving.
And up North somewhere, someone is dreaming the Fender bass.
While across Texas, Black men in shiny tuxedos,
cotton shirts sticking to their skinny torsos,
rise and fall to the beat, the backbeat. A faster shuffle.
A wilder vamp. The beboppers are intellectual, you know,
and fast too. And everyone gets into the aviary act.
Flamingos, Orioles, rocking . Just waiting, just waiting to grind you
        home.

Was it the teasing power of Big Boy Crudup or Ruth Brown's
haughty insinuations or the crazy men in Macon with their too tight

suit pants and dicks as long as legend permits.
Was it Aretha in the womb listening to Mahalia crooning
and Otis tossing footballs as the marching bands practiced
across the wide fields of the fifties South? Was it ever
so easy to make a voice that seduced and soothed as much as Etta
      James's,
who was pretty as Billie, and soon strung out too.

What made these people, Southern mostly, Black absolutely,
churn up rhythms rich as currents in the Atlantic?

Was it Billie standing in that pool of ugly light?
Fair skin wrinkling. Desperate for the ease of a needle.
Was it ever as sad as this? Not even the grave yet.
Eight more years before the coffin's fit to surround her.
And the men like hellcats cursing the click of her expensive heels.
Soft stone in her pocket. Rhinestones in her earlobes.
The dope man's leash shorter and shorter each time the world
      begged for more.

Billie shivers in her skin going slack. Joking the dope down.
Her face maps a bitter terrain.
From pain and back again.
While each door that opens for her, closes.
But now, this moment, the door opens, a crack
where the light bleeds in, stays on her, merciless.

On the lonely roads in Arkansas, Mississippi, Tennessee
and Texas, skinny men in too tight pants shook out the blues.
And up in Chicago, someone with a harmonica wailed and wailed
I WANT YOU I WANT YOU I WANT YOU

and out of all the stars that fell on Alabama, Little Richard flipped
out of his melodrama and made this scream. His pomaded hair
flinging greasy love to the adoring girls giggling in the
background.

Wailing like the caped saxophone players and the gutbucket
        guitarists,
like the women with Big in front of their names—Mama,
Maybelle-
relentless. Somewhere before the spotlight lengthened
to include so many, so beautiful, so always
rocking rocking rocking till the break of dawn.
Was it ever easy this motion of blood and mucus and dream?
First born and angry at the given world.
A noble operation for Caesar used for a poor Black woman
already wanting to break this wall, as hand claps break a forest's
silence. Uterine wall collapsing,
so they cut my mother's belly and drag me out
wailing too.

In Like Paradise/Out Like the Blues

1.

huddled over his acoustic guitar, he heard voices from the center of
     the earth
(sonorous revolutions per minute transmitting)
MUTANT MUTANT
You've fooled around too long.

2.

After Rufino Tamayo returned from mapping
the Cosmos, he turned to his wife and said

Stars are like flowers in the desert.
They shiver fresh in the aeon knowing
that they will become memory, hunger,
the core of dreams.

It is up to me, then, to bring back their beauty:
taut, seamless before the eyes of men and women.
To amplify the vitality of their illumination
(righteous shimmer above melancholy clouds)
To remind humanity that without them night would never come.

3.

The death of a star like the death of a flower
Is awesome, ugly, a relentless warning.

4.

Artists make whole somehow the ways
In which dreams persist.

Each of us turns to the hunger of stars
And wipes the crumbs from our mouths.

On canvas, they laugh like children.
In essence, they scream like children.
And struggle like children to eat, grow, copulate, then flash out.
A name perhaps. A body gone.

5.

Heeding the wails of heaven-frenzy
of hard-loved electric guitars—he removed
the soft strings from his life, one by one.
He replaced each of them with fool's silver.
Steel. Blueheated. Oxidized.
Glistening. Sweat like gold rivers flowing
down the face of a man black as the hunger of stars.

His urgent guitar flaming
His body hungry hungry hungry
Cocaine/methedrine
Slim women hovering about him, specters.
Thirsty. He is weeping.
Some thing got lost.
A man who plays fire never stays to dinner.
Is welcome in the house of the living only so long.
And then there are the photographs, the videos.
Gossip. Memorabilia.

Songs on the radio at tender hours—five past
midnight or three A.M.

The death of one so young is angry.
A sin perhaps. Dust. Secrets. Forever. Gone.

6.

You've got to know when you're weary.
So you will lie down and rest.

You've got to know when you're weary.
So you'll lie down and rest.

If you take your dreams serious
You may get yourself blessed.

7.

Like legacy. Like Paradise.
Like the crushed perfume of a captive flower.
Like the notation of your very first breath
Like memory

Like the cradle rocking in the heart of a poet
back and forth
back and forth

you've got to know when you're weary
so you will lie down and rest.

Encounter and Farewell

It's all foreplay, really-this walk
through the French Quarter exploring souvenir shops,
each of them carefully deranged, as if dust were to settle
only at perfect intervals. Yes to the vetiver fan
that smells sweeter than sandalwood or cedar.
No to the mammy doll dinner bells.
No to the mammy dolls whose sewn smiles are as fixed
as the lives of too many poor Black women here:
motherhood at twelve, drugged, abandoned by fifteen,
dead by twenty (suicide, murder) so easily in Desire.
And yet, their voices sweeten the snaking air,
providing the transvestites their proper Muses,
all of whom have streets named for them in the Garden District.

A soft heat settles on Terpsichore,
just inside the gay bar where the owner's pink flamingos
complement silly songs on the rescued Rockola.
Who can dance to that Lorne Greene ballad, "Ringo"?

Dixie beer is the beer of choice; marijuana the cheapest drug.
Relaxation is key, since it's all a matter of waiting
for the right body to stumble toward you.
Lust perfumes parties in the projects, barstool chatter at the Hyatt,
lazy kissing on the median strip stretching down Tchoupitoulas.
If Professor Longhair were alive, he'd teach a lesson
in seamless motion: the perfect slide of a man's hand down a
            woman's back;

a lesson you learned long ago before you met me. We are making love
as we did before in Austin and Manhattan.
But in this room on this costly bed our lovemaking
starts out the slowest grind, then, like this city's weather,
goes from hot to hotter, from moist to rainstorm wet.

You're tall, A., and where there should be tribal markings
there are scars-football, basketball, mid-sixties grind parties
where something always got out of hand. There's the perfect
amen. You're your own gospel.
And you bring good news to me-the way you enter me
Like grace, the way you say my name, a psalm.
No. That's not it. It's the engineer in you that
gets me. Your search for the secret line that goes
straight to the center of the earth. Deeper and deeper
you go until there's no earth left in me. And we
hum and moan a song as old as our selves gone back.

There are too many souvenirs in your eyes.
Gifts given too often, too hastily, never opened.

Outside a city sprawls its heat, seeks out every pore,
licks every moment of sweat as we shiver in this chilly room
taking each other's measure. We say good-bye again and again.
As if every kiss, every touch we make will shadow
All our celebrations.

And they do.

If I Were Rita Hayworth

I would hear Spanish first.
My father would teach me how to shimmer.
My mother would keep her mouth shut.

I would wear red dresses at age 12
and dance like a woman many years older.
I would dance in my father's arms.

Later I would dye my hair red
and pluck the last Spanish words from my mouth.

I would masquerade as an American
that healthy girl next door who knows
how to crack a whip.

I would dream only in black and white
(after Technicolor, some peace is needed).

As the Studio built a whole world for me
full of fresh cream and gingerbread, I would seek
out the darkest men, nigger dark, then fuck them
into marriage. I would wed a Prince of Darkness
and bear daughters named for the perfumes of Arabia.

If l were Rita Hayworth, strung between living a lie
and bearing a sickness so furious it ages me to dream of it,
I would rage in my illness, make a black hole
wide enough to swallow the damnation of my beauty.

The Usual Suspect

From the Billie Holiday Chronicles

Satin gown the color of black sand under full moonlight.
Voice colored jewel rich. Ruby rouge. Cat's-eye
green. Blue at autumn twilight blue.
She's got this big sad heart.
When she sings, she sings the world's real dream:
love, faith, money.
The world's real problem: love, fear, death.

She's gorgeous. Full storm . NO WARNING
Her voice sweeps couples together.
It is that real weather
that kills and kills
and makes the day so new.

She tells a thousand stories-no, one thousand and one.
A Scheherazade night after night, conjuring her dreams.
So the torchlights flame in the street
and blood rushes pell-mell from heart to lung to feet.
Every bent note spins like a ballroom's gaudy globe
on an axis of hope: that tomorrow the fly figure
of a pomaded man will make the troubles glow away.
Life, as always, is too real now-
battles over there; the lynch-throated barefoot man, here.
Flag-draped coffins traveling to segregated cemeteries
while colored troops guarding German rows beg to hear Lena
        Horne.

It's a gambler's moon, the troop trains' keen departures.
So elegant this grand weeping beneath vaulted ceilings
in cities with Indian names, where old men sell whatever
takes away the worry: massively floral perfumes,
cheap Havanas and cheaper reefer, and the latest recordings
of a woman fragrant with gardenia blossoms,

tobacco and Florida water. There are times when only the spring
in her throat offers the essential prayers.
And even then, the world trips, stumbles and falls away
from her voice as if deaf, dumb and blind.

San Francisco, Spring 1986

I feel so East Coast. Shut down, frantic.
Too used to the expensive, the hot-house flowers sold on
every corner. Here the flowers brighten every corner. Free.
Here, the wildflowers are different. Calla lilies grow wild?
Silky, white, trumpet, shaped, composed,

As is this midday light.
Translucent in the Embarcadero.
White, hot, harsh in the Mission.
There, the pink, gray and yellow stucco houses
shutter themselves against the brutal splendor.

As I and Roberto sip beer and talk poetry, politics, the growing list
of men with AIDS, heat is almost forgotten in the midday darkness
of this Salvadoran restaurant.
We patrons linger over plates of rice and beans, vivid spices
harry our hunger as the beers splash down our throats.

This cool seems dreamlike.
Our meal timeless.
But time does matter.

Men here, lovers, friends, are
learning women's work.
The weary labor of mothers ,sisters, aunts.

How many pills? Can we afford this?
Here's the doctor's private number.
All the statements that pave the way
for rest, guilt and more work
with someone else.

Here's where the caring begins. Here's where
the caring works. Even as lovers defiantly declare,

"I know he's dying. I won 't get tested.
Not just yet."

Here's where the time is taken.
Here's where the story matters.
Where the weeping and the anger commence.

As if the hard-bodied men
so very young in the Castro,
enterprising in the Haight,
discreet in the Mission
compose an army fighting blind.

And who could be blind to this city's beauty?
Where century-old eucalyptus rend
cathedrals before stone and the sun's lush glow
halos the rise and fall of exhausted hills

What is so easily available here—the green coast
and an ocean at war with its name—is not so easily
taken away.
These men dying are not given up without love,
without caring, without a fight

Baby Hair Shirt

here is a conventional dress pattern
short sleeves, high waist, slightly flaring skirt
if this dress could swing as dresses do in summer
it would swing with the best of them
but this is not a dress

it is made of handmade paper
stained by black tea
veined by human hair

not the infant's fine hair
but thick, heavy strands
that twines through the dress
like veins beneath a baby's skin
exposed, a living highway

this dress form is as stiff
as the one worn by the Infanta
in that portrait by Velázquez

La Infanta, baby princess
stands poised, ladylike, prepared
to assume her considerable privilege as infant
as royalty
as daughter of the ugliest king in Europe

who sits astride numinous stallions
as the Inquisition strips away the flesh of the sinful
the intellectual
the Jews and the Moors
whose hair has not the fine, lank texture
of the king's coiffure

but whose ideas have a power even Velázquez recognizes,
secretes in his shadowy portraits of Philip and his family

His harsh brushstrokes comb the pointed beard
of the regent, streak the soft folds of the Infanta's
silk dress, catch the sour breath of a dying empire

as does Chrysanne's miniature dress

that types the wearer (if there was a wearer)
surrounds her in a token of pain

not the first hard thrust into life's bright air
but the daily material that makes a life being lived

choices and consequences pinching the nerve spirit over flesh
joy or despair
love or the dream of it
pricking the skin, dancing in the veins

mocking the girl's goodness
making the grim details of the baby's growing up
a laughing matter like cancer of the esophagus
or a shotgun blast to the heart

for Chrysanne Stathacos and Paloma Hagedorn Woo

Glad All Over

I saw Julian Bond in 1965 at a SNCC rally,
just outside this shack on the side of town where I was not supposed
            to be.
It was even poorer than where I lived.
I was curious. Everyone was curious.
This was about organizing. But were we ready?
As ready as Black folk in West Memphis, Marianna,
Helena. Up and down the Delta. Was it so bad
that there could be no turning back?

In a mythic retelling, I could say I joined SNCC,
attended every meeting, rallied all my friends,
marched every march.
But mothers have eyes and ears everywhere in small towns
and mine found out.
She wanted change as bad as she wanted the schools integrated,
hot running water in our house, a car loan paid off,
and a husband who did more than scream at her daily
before he went to wherever he worked. But first
things first. I, eldest daughter. She, working mother.
No contest. At home I had to watch my brother and sister.
Tend to the house falling down. Some of my classmates marched
to the center of the city, were jailed. A boycott began.
It seemed as fit failed, this boycott.
But downtown was dying since Black folk weren't buying.
The Chamber of Commerce refused to say it was so.

It seemed as if nothing changed. For a while, I stood
on the sidelines as those becoming mythic figures of history
crashed by. Until the day Arkansas state troopers stood
in the front of my mother's house, high-powered rifles aimed
at the people on my street-my childhood in gun sight.
This after our neighbors—a father and two sons were arrested
by the corrupt sheriff, taken to jail, then released to the waiting

Klan. They got out alive, but only after broken collarbones, broken
legs, hemorrhages, bruises, contusions, stomped-on dreams.
I see my mother, who until that day could not say shit,
go up to one of the troopers and politely, quietly demand:
"Sir, see these children. Please lower your rifle."
He did.

Later that night, every house in my neighborhood stood ready.
The only lights visible were streetlamps.
My brother and a friend sat on our front porch,
loaded shotguns in their laps. Waiting, waiting for any white man
to come down Division Street. Inside our house, my mother prayed,
and I started this poem that only begins to grasp my mother's feat,
our family's ordinary courage.

It's hard to see children in T-shirts that read "Any Means Necessary"
and know that they have not sat as my brother
sat on a porch with a rifle waiting, just waiting to kill
any white man fool enough
to be a member of the Klan.

So, yes, we did not all meet the fire hoses in Birmingham,
or face down Chicago police in a battle for the hearts and minds
of suburbanites fearful that Fred Hampton, George Jackson,
even the dead Martin Luther King would disturb their manicured
lawns.
"Glad all over" bubbles up, the secret joy beneath grim
turbulence
of a decade now known as much for the pursuit of pleasure as for
political assassination, a war broadcast nightly, lawless police,
ritual murder and hard, harsh truths. Getting harder.

The Perfect Lipstick

When the life-sized replicas of the *Nina*,
the *Pinta*, and the *Santa Maria*
precariously sailed into New York harbor,
they looked like toy ships.

Just think, Columbus in a toy ship.
Off to discover the perfect route-
the fastest way to China, the Indies,
all that spice.

He never got this far north.
But all the same, the slaughter of whole peoples,
buildings that even God had not thought of in 1492,
and "expulsion," "discovery," the "Slave Trade"
all followed.

Out of this horror came new foods
new clothes new shoes
a language as mixed as the blood of the people
and as alienating.

But there are times when the connections, no matter how fragile,
hold, like the thick sails of those tall ships
which decorated the harbor July 4 in fog and gentle light.

It is why I appreciate my favorite shade of lipstick:
Sherry Velour.

Sounds like the name of a drag queen from the early seventies.
One of those strapping Black men who had enough of playing
         macho,
put their feet in five-inch heels and made saints of Dinah
         Washington,
Rita Hayworth and a very young Nina Simone.

So, on goes this lipstick. Pretty for parties.
Fatal for festivals.
Sherry Velour and her hot discoveries:
light above the fog,
a toy ship.
Black men in sequined dresses and the click of new words
in the new world where the most dangerous of dreams
come true.

Sly & The Family Stone Under the Big Tit/Atlanta, 1973

We waited and waited. Stoned for Sly. Southern sons and daughters
of the Rainbow Tribe. Under Georgia Tech' Big Tit's Big Tit.
Sucking in the marijuana, blowing out the heat.

Former debs with shag cuts and torn jeans their good old boy
friends who used to hunt and fish, now glitter-rocked, ready
with red painted nails and the latest Mott the Hoople tape
on their dashboards. Rebel boys back from 'Nam who used
to party with the brothers on the DMZ-that is, when they
were not beating the shit out of each other before the
vc struck up yet another victorious attack.

Sly's the perfect foil for this crowd.
"Sex Machine" and "Don't Call Me Nigger, Whitey" are
our anthems of choice. "I want to take you higher" just seems like
dessert. And of course, Sly is late.
Real late. Sly may not even be in the vicinity.
Like the airport.

Then the house lights actually dim.
The band comes out ragged. Like every musician from Provence to
        Paducah,
they have to play, but their bodies droop. Their songs droop.
And Sly appears indeed to be stoned. By this time the audience
could care less. The show would've gone on. We could sing
this shit.
We could take the stage and trash it. We could suck beers and colas
till the aluminum disappeared.

This is the end of the mighty rainbow. The brothers in huge Afros,
amulets and attitudes stalk the round of the Big Tit, checking,
        checking
everybody out. And blond boys with open paisley shirts
parade their chest hair

and tight pants so many peacocks, while we girls
just catch the magnificent promenade.
Between the air outside and the air in here,
there are worlds galore. And we want it all.

The Rainbow Tribe picks up the mess of miscegenation,
our cluttered history, and walks outside.
Into the Georgia night. Fucked up and full of spleen.
Ripped off, someone yells.
But we all had a good time. Really.
Waiting for the California soul sound
to wash over us like an ocean wave,
like something we've dreamed about but
could not hear. Like a song of peace.

Sly Stone under the Big Tit, pretty in that messy-colored California
            way.
Making music happen while the lights in his eyes dimmed.

And we too wanted to make something work that couldn't.
The sex machine switched off.
The highs were plummeting.
An avalanche of choices awaiting all of us.

But all we wanted was to party. To mess around with the mess
            around.
To shift ourselves out of the Georgia sun-stroked days
and turn into each other's arms as Family,
and loving always loving the way we thought the world should be.

5:25 A.M.

You're not a saxophone
key of permanent blue
nor toe plumed serpent electric guitar
come to breakfast on fire

Into storms that shift invisible
your voice grounds deep
in the wake of something new.
(That's why the light burns in the bathroom.)

The weight of you
is traced on my sheets by musk, semen
oil of coconut (your hair).

An African profile hardened into that dance
the old one where shoulders lean
into cracks between Motown harmonies.
(That's why the stereo's too loud.)

And what you mean, the African-American dream:
he was smart
so he walked
as if he
was going somewhere
important.
(That's why the buses are late.)

Around you always this halo of music
a song so sweet, it makes teeth ache.

for Robert

Thief's Song

In this film, Neruda defends a young poet's
theft of his metaphors.

A young woman rolls an egg
across her generous breast.

Everyone speaks Spanish
as the jukebox plays the Beatles' version
of "Please Mr. Postman."

Off camera, President Allende dies
an ugly, dangerous death.

Allende's ideas are tossed about,
many shells in a relentless storm.

Then the film follows Neruda's sad decline:
his feet upon rocky terrain,
eyes on miraculous water.

Solitude: heart of eternal fire.
Psalm: bridge between dream and sky.

for Thulani Davis

Measure

In the traffic jam on the way to the picnic
I think of the Julio Cortázar short story.
Probably inspired by Godard's *Weekend* or maybe
he was trapped on the highway just outside Paris
for five hours of what was a 40-minute trip.
Minutes do not flash by or crawl, they tick.
Off toward destination-there is this little panic
are we going in the right direction?

On the beach, I ask Dan and Nick how wide is Lake Tahoe.
Nick recoils from the question, looks at Dan and says:
"Why do women ask us these questions?
Don't they know we just make it up as we go along."
Dan nods, agreeing. He smiles.
"3.72 miles and the mountains are . . ."
"I know," I say. "It's all improvisation."

The scientists that Carrie McCray describes in her notes
for a poem on Ota Benga come to mind.
How they measured his skull, digits, his penis
in search of what they desired: "The Missing Link."
Or Elizabeth Alexander's calculated retelling of the story of "The
        Venus
Hottentot," who was treated as a curiosity, her sex exposed.

Could it be that ease with ticking off the length of an ear,
the abacus' computation
the span of the measuring stick
the tape measure sprung,
then recoiled that makes women ask
how much
how many
how long

Connecting quantifiable time and distance is as dumbfounded
as the stars' lunatic mapmaking.
Or so it seemed the night I was drunk enough
to apprehend the shape of Orion's Belt.
I was blessed, puzzled.

Why can't I swing Orion's Belt around my waist
and dance that dance that starts and stops the cosmic traffic?
Why can't you?

We are stuck on this ground. In this traffic. On this beach.
Dry grasses bend beneath the weight of our feet.
And the hummingbird's flight stops conversation,
a mark in summer air.

Why these wet lawns full of grasses, insects, budding flowers
whose names we are to call?

We look across the lake. The mountains tremble
at an immeasurable speed.
And we have nothing to do with it.

What the God of Fire Charged Me

Pague lo que el dios defuego / me cobro
—Ana Ilce

Each turn is the one that mocks
the old order and when the revolution happens
another readies itself.
Like the surge of blood in spring
or the lost hope of a winter
where kisses were too few or too many.

You will say, "She's romantic."
And you will be correct.
But one dimension is only one dimension.
The others remain unseen.
Be wary.

When the night watch ends
and the sun rises—a smile on land and water
I worry less about the dreams I cannot suppress
but more about the life
I am so willing to live.

One turn, then the other.
A fire walk as prelude.
A dance best forgiven.

New Blues

In bolder times, I'd be knee-deep in trouble:
kissing the brow of some dark-skinned dream of a man
or floating off the blasted brass in a smoky loft-draped
in silk-smooth cotton. But it's midnight in Dorchester, and
Robert Cray emphatically sings about wanting no more
of whatever was there before the song had to be sung.

It's a sad song. Funny, too. Hellhounds chased Robert Johnson
from one end of the Delta to the other.
But this singer's problem is much more local.
He just wants his lover to move out. Property is the new devil.
Who owns the lease gets to live. And sing about it.

Yes, the blues changes. Taught like economics or post-war poetry-
fussed over like a cranky aunt with money to leave behind.
Amusing and serious, this robust American tradition.
The blues and its borders.

In the movies, it gets very, very odd.
See *The Birth of the Blues*, in which Bing Crosby
and the boys create Dixieland jazz and take it from New Orleans
to Chicago.
Eddie "Rochester" Anderson is there to add a note of authenticity.
And Mary Martin is the "chick" singer.

The journey is drenched in glorious moonlight in front of black and
            white
mattes designed by somebody German (probably).
As the boys (all white, mind you, except dear Rochester) cheerfully
            play and fight,
"darkies" on the shore pick cotton, drink corn liquor, get lynched
and add to the exotic atmosphere.
A lone curl of smoke rises from a shack's

miserable chimney. Rochester wields his broom like a bayonet
as he escorts Miss Martin across the bridge between comic relief
and the lonesome, heartless voice of a blues man conjuring revenge.

After that, I ask, is there room for such cinematic loss in the New
        Blues?
Where are those hellhounds, loose ends: women, whiskey bottle
        gone dry,
the sheriff from the next county coming to yours, that slap kick in
        the groin
after midnight and before the wolf's sad hour?

The pawnshops of memory are closed now. And some women refuse
        to slice
one more cheek over one last goodtime man. What to do?

When the last train whistle rasps, and only the jet's sonic boom
dazzles, will the drum kit slit the air and the saxophone
bends down so low
someone checks their back pockets as the guitar strips away
one more story: the one about the man and the woman,
the one about standing at the bridge,
the one told on the mockingbird's tongue
in a voice that scrapes the geologic layers of modern times
as if it could reveal the origins of the race.

But this morning, Cray's voice crawls off the phonograph,
a snake hungry for the future.
And I make one more cup of coffee, read critical theory,
then start to follow
the slithering line from ear to heart,
then back to the clock against the wall.

from FEMME DU MONDE

Hope, Arkansas, 1970

A wealthy white man drives up to the golden arches—Texas plates.
It's a Mercedes sedan, luxuriantly glistening. And from the
      passenger side,
emerges a blonde child, made up—tarted up, as a Brit would say.

We were freshmen girls on the way to our suitemate's wedding.
Starting out from Memphis, the Mississippi whipping up currents,
we've crossed Arkansas from East to West—Dallas our destination.

We sung silly songs to curb Nancy's fear of crossing bridges to
a smiling hatred of girls singing off-key, raucously. It worked. We're
      here.
But, who is this man to this child? Father, lover, dirty old uncle.

We put down our milkshakes, sandwiches and fries.
The little blonde chatters away. The man strokes her hand.
The girls we are become womanly, matronly.
We want to rescue this child.

But where would we take her?
And what would happen to all that money?

for Nancy Howell

Ghosts

He was filled with beauty, so filled he could not stop the shadows
from their walk around his horn, blasting cobwebs in the Fillmore's
     ceiling

Somewhere dawn makes up for the night before, but he is floating.
Dead in the water. And yet, my lover tells me, he saw him
     shimmering.

As did others. It could have been the acid. Or fragmented
     harmonics.
His reed ancestral. This perilous knowledge. The band went home,

shivering. A girl threw roses in the water. Carnations, daisies. And
     bright red sashes.
Like ones the Chinese use for funeral banners. A drummer intoned
     chants

From the Orient. Police wrote up the news. Years later, my lover told
     me
Friends would hear the whisper, then a tone, full throttle from the
     wind.

Ghosts on Second Avenue, jazzmen in the falling stars.
If you catch one, your hands will glitter.

Comme des Garçons

The Italians really know how to do red,
now it is the Japanese.
Poised on poured concrete, this vivid scarlet
expensively, carefully cut, harlot,
silk as parachute.

A midnight purple velvet brushes the hand
catlike as if in conversation with the silk.
Persian versus Siamese?

A chaste white slithers the length of mannequins
oddly shaped as if female form is an afterthought.

Under the stern lights suave white floats a line
of solitude, crystalline as first snowfall,
forgetful of the swift human charge
that takes to pulling threads from the elaborately
disguised seams, splatters white water,
scars every attempt at human perfection.

Like this green jacket suddenly male.
Will the actor buy it?
Will it work for all the other boys?

Ascending the brutal staircases towards
chaste white and harlot red, lipstick luscious,

what matters if the forms dematerialize leaving sex,
solitude, and the frank shapes of credit for contemplation.

Elsewhere, all is feline.

On my favorite episode of *Amos 'n' Andy*, Kingfish comes home with found money, lots of it and says to his wife, Sapphire: "I've always promised to bring home the bacon. Well, honey, I brought you the whole hog."

Sapphire

I swore to a friend that yes, you can live on martinis and chocolate!
Dark chocolate, real chocolate, slightly bitter and lovely to smell.

And it helps to have a working knowledge of languages other than
       English:
French, perhaps German or Spanish.
This will serve one well from Brussels to Krakow.

Entertain your learned hosts. Toss in expertise, opinion, and artful
       snobbery.
Baraka and Yeats, poetry, theater, cultural inquiry, any good reason
       to party.
Well, party on. What a swank notion, the Black sophisticate
with a working knowledge of Celtic mythology and hoodoo, shouts
       and blues.

Sophisticated lady. Walking this tensile rope that swings between
       pocketbook and fantasy.
This side Paradise. That side bankruptcy.
Who cares if the woods are scary, dark and deep?
German food is gray, white and green, the sausages brown.
Winter food. Winter people.

The Lenbachhaus empty but for the curator, an interpreter and me.
       We walk at a pace
known only to museum workers—respectful, professional, with time
       enough for the surprise,
the find, a reverent glance. There is danger here and dedication.

Franz Marc's fantastic horses swirling reds, yellows, an impossible
    purplish blue.
Read birth dates and death notices. World War I—destroyer of
    artists.

There is our heroine. The girlfriend or wife who will not sacrifice
one measure of her talent even as her beloved recoils
from his promise of a perfect union made in art.

Left at the train station, in an airport, on the side of the road,
women have always been wise to scrap and savvy composing
canvasses of prodigious color and luminosity. It is not always

night in our soul of souls. Just a weak ache for what could have
    been.
We were raised to recognize the brute's soft smile and the trickster's
    violent craft, but
not the tender one's evolving desire, his roving eye, his voice
    crashing against our tears.

Who is to blame? The ideal of it all. Gabriele Münter stopped not
    once the making of
her art. How could she, when her lover stopped not the making of
    his, only his love for her.

Blue, blue, blue rider. *Der Blaue Reiter* sees what you have left
    behind.
Paintings dance and marvel, assume aspects of magic, prophecy,
    precision and dread.
Iron works forged a martial steel. Gunpowder, dynamite, munitions,
    munificence.

And yes, she hid from the Nationalist Socialists remnants of prewar
    experiments
essaying the values of colors, shapes, the artists' place beneath the
    dismal stars to come.

This is how the story spends itself, late twentieth century on the
        wide
boulevards of great European cities where the dust and trouble
of war and revival stratify the effortless rebuilding.

A plaque in the plaza marking a speech, a battle, the death of one
        great man
or a tribe's lonely disaster. Rings of fire or rings of gold.
Sooner or later a story unfolds.

What matters is that I stood there, three days before Palm Sunday,
        1989
eyeing the elaborate chocolate rabbits in the window of a Munich
        confectioner.

The sweet hare's fabled face-whiskers shiver in the icy breeze of air
        conditioning.
His ears proportioned, listening for our appreciation.

You really want panic? Think of the chocolatier's skill.
How for every perfect bunny in the window,
hundreds lie in pieces awaiting his children's ready mouths.

Ah, the kids get the damaged goods for that is the way of the world.
And they lick the brutalized ears with much joy.

Shack with Vines

Who lives in this motley house?
Some old woman left back of
the bottom of the county.

She's crazy. No, she's poor.
She makes her taste of something
as bitter as the broad leaves

choking the last of life from her house.

Did she go to church each Sunday?
Pull the yellow streamers during the Maypole dance?
Learn the first four chapters of Genesis
by the age of nine?

Where is her family?
Or was there not a family?
Did she nurse the folk of the county?
Is this the conjure woman, so talked about?

Or is the resident of this dying house male?
Shotgun at his bedside, ready
to blast aside the wicked.

This is his sanctuary, this little house.
Away from the highway,
far outside of town.

Far from the many temptations of the flesh,
about which he reads repeatedly in weak daylight.

Or are there orphaned children sleeping beneath blankets,
coats, whatever warmth was left behind?
They remember electricity, hot showers, macaroni and cheese.

Scavengers in the town, their T-shirts, old jeans,
and itchy, unwashed sweaters contour skinny backs.
There they are outside the local fast food drive-in

sifting through the cast off bread and meat,
laughter tossed over the bin like an acidulent anecdote.

Shack collapsing.

Why I Left the Country: A Suite

The Suburban Dream

The house could be anywhere—desert, valley,
mountainside—lucre and luck find the site.

There is much told pleasure culled from the perfected house.
Sniff the floorboards, stroke the gold and brass fixtures, slide fingers
along suave countertops, behold high ceiling's profligate beams,
drape the snake-coiled cosmology of infrastructure across the architect's
drafting table.

Dream the developer's glossy dream.
Delight in worlds produced with pencils, hammers, paper and glass.

You'd think this wonderful.
You'd be suburban.

A Gallant History

The austerity of luxuriant rural life can be spiteful.
On neighbors' properties, orphaned dogs
and uncompromising cats rant flagrant music
as they plunder garbage and rachet trees.

A full moon limns a vigil for the dream house:
tales of bourbon bottles stashed behind the bronze umbrella stand;
a garden hoe used to discipline an errant servant
who flirtatious said "Good morning" to the madam who swooned;
frayed velvet and satin ribbons colored rouge, silver, opal and gold
gird the rotting love letters of long dead maiden aunts;
unbleached yellowed stains on the maid's narrow mattress
the whispered "No" unheard.

Where are the wildflowers and the humdrum magic of tea?

The City Proper

The crosstown bus is due any minute.
Satisfied commuters stoop to lift bags of carefully purchased stuff:
costumes for the latest wave in carnival fêtes;
cosmetics for a firmer face and thigh;
jewels for passing about in private.
A lucent fire.

Dinner is picaresque.
A tableau of gestures in the making of feasts.
Lemongrass, cilantro, hominy, wine.
At midnight, everyone is exhausted in town
and out.

One minute past the witching hour, where is that divine waiter?
He forgot to bring my check.

The Village Sparkles

In German, *Vagina* is always capitalized.
It is subject, therefore, important.

In America, who knows what is important.
Julia Roberts or Vagina or Julia Roberts and Vagina.

Actually, this is a dodge. My hand hurts.
My heart aches. Intemperate spices breach summer air

and yet, I blush. Nutmeg, cinnamon. Who can handle Spring or
Penis in Winter. Cardamom, Ginger. Garlic for Luck.

Who cares about Dream?
Important, subject.

Action. Where is action? If we weep too much,
we go crazy. If we don't weep, we go crazy.

Crazy, he calls me. What a great line.
Willie Nelson looks like tobacco spit in snow.

But what a great line. Crazy, who calls me crazy?
The one I want hollers for me, STELLA
STELLA walking the floors, diva in the making,
clicking my Italian boots' steel-edged heels.

Vagina or Vocation. Vaginal, vocational
Love or Lust or Limits at the gas station.

Everything reckons on days when heaven releases perfume.
Come claim my loving heart, I call to him.

I want you funny and hungry
and wrinkled with sweat.

Sunday morning, after Church
the Village sparkles. I tell a good friend.
You know, I can smell men.

for Susan Wheeler

Saltimbanque

That there is a place of art in the city and society, the space allowed to art, its different guises and its very different publics, its perversions in the courts and its suppression in the streets.

—T. J. Clarke, *The Absolute Bourgeois: Artists and Politics in France 1848–1851*

1.

Suppose Daumier had behaved differently? His walks across
Paris uneventful. News banal—barricades, congresses,
the secret societies ineffectual. What would his cartoons reveal?
The fat bellied bourgeois slimmer? The masses
stepping into well-made shoes?
Or would he have— as he did in private— made more paintings
of the *saltimbanques*: street performers suppressed,
by order of the State?

Were their songs too political, pornographic?
Had their children not received instruction from the priests?
Were their dancing dogs and wily monkeys better off
burned?

Have we not enough water?
Is there not enough air?

2.

Banners dirty and torn, fragmented song singes air.
Why are the revolutions of 1848 present?
Weapons in the hands of peasants, slave rebellions
in the American South, the monarchy in crisis,
plutocrats measure their new-found power in gilt, silk, velocity.

Pamphleteers for the right hand and the left.
Militarists, Marx, and monopoly capitalists,
the modern world embryonic.

3.

What a blaze was to be made in less than one hundred years.
Sorting through shadows, airborne war machines
disrupt, destroy with electrical ease.
An eleven-year-old's voice is suddenly burdened
with dust,
human dust as ovens roars a clinical heat.
(Attendants weep as a passage from Wagner rises
from a well-tended Victrola.)
Displaced, disloved, dissolved almost,
a patch of khaki becomes a small girl's dress,
old shoelaces are ribbons for her hair.
A population of zombies begs for cigarettes and curse.

4.

On a Saigon street, in the midday heat
or so it seems in the black and white film
a Buddhist monk in a moment
of amazing rage and pure tenderness
doused his saffron robes.
We do not see this vivid yellow.
We taste dust. Human dust.

Sous les pavés, la plage
Under the pavement, the beach.

5.
Sous les pavés, la plage
Songs of freedom scorch parched throats.
Workers and students defy enforced alienation.
Rise together, spray police with pamphlets, curses,
on the very paving stones that once were danced upon
by the *saltimbanques*, their children and trained beasts.
While an ocean away, under an image of the ever-defiant Che,

intellectuals, idealists, the disaffected rallied across
a hemisphere. In the mountains of Central America,
poets purged themselves in clear, cold streams,
debated desire, and learned to shoot.
Sous les pavés, la plage.

6.

On a road to Biafra, in the slums of Manila,
on the back streets of Kingston, inside the chain-linked lawns
of South Los Angeles, people make a song, new song, riot song
as a stockpile of promises collapses the shanty towns,
miners' camps, the migrant workers' buses traveling north
from Florida seats sticky with overripe oranges.

Under the pavement, the beach.
Under a stockpile of rotting promises, human stench
Bodies gunned down in daylight in Manila, Mexico City,
Memphis, Tennessee. Cameras chasing children
grabbing a solid taste of fire.

And earlier that year, Soviet tanks pressed against
the Prague Spring, a winter storm drowning flowers.

7.

Martin King sat bleeding in a Birmingham jail. He worked
his mind along the sacred stations of the cross and found,
if not solace, then the tattered cloth called dignity,
as he prayed for the souls of his jailers.

Tracing Alabama dust, his cross just heavy enough to bear,
Word could have been miracle, joy, power.
It was likely to have been song, people, or alone.

He made, in private, a face mimicking the fat, snuff-dipping guards.
Clown face turned towards jail-floor dust.
His tears roll away holy laughter. *Saltimbanque*
in a moment of amazing tenderness and pure rage.

Under the paving stones, the beach.

Natalie Schmidt contributed the French phrases created by the Situationists from the May 1968 Student Protests in Paris

All Saints' Day

Diamanda Galas screams sings
rage upon love
as winter forms
drop by cooling drop.

And earlier in that year, spring in the Blue Ridge—
pastures and hills bejeweled
with violets, dogwoods, the Judas Tree—
softens the bitter taste
of recipes for worming, for worry,
for the death of masters, overseers,
the uniformed patriarchs of a history
astonished by defeat. The burned mansions and
moth-ridden grief come back to haunt lanes
to the left and right, a clear divide

between the Black side and the white.
On All Saints' Day, a wind resurrected
as dervish, spiraling dry, sharp leaves

righteous fuel for bonfires.
Honorable music to comfort the dead.

My Matthew Shepard Poem

My students are rightfully spooked
someone their age was left to perish
because he preferred the company of men

My mother tells me of seeing a man lynched
back in the 30's, in Arkansas, not far from where
I grew up and grew away in the 60's.

What I know about America is that hatred
crawls through the culture like the cracks
in the San Andreas fault.

Edifices are built to withstand the inevitable
quakes, but the quakes grow stronger.
Whatever we dream harmony or a reasonable tolerance
is destroyed in the wake

of men drinking and killing. Their blood lusted
laughter howling through the night.

A Black man in Texas. A white man in Wyoming.
A doctor at his window about to eat dinner with his family.
A nurse on her way to work at a clinic.

The playing field is not level. In fact, there is no playing field.
There are men enraged by change. And women bitter about it.
And people, say
gay, Black, Latino, Chinese, Japanese, Arab, or Jewish
to blame, always to blame.

The men in their same wool suits and striped ties
gibber political correctness, freedom, fairness
and fuck you

every time they claim that these are acts of individuals, not of
        society.
Each act alone represents

singular aberrant behavior, like murder.
I can hear them say, I mean they actually lynched that boy,
even as they call this one faggot and that one nigger.
And they really, really want women
compliant and girlish
or sexless and mothering.

And if this seems like male bashing, so be it.
If the dress shoe fits, may it pinch like hell.

Laura

The most beautiful woman in the room nailed to a wall.

Her prim confidante laments the death of goddesses.
His is a feline recollection—the sibilant sound of her voice,
the droop of her eyelids; the dynamic wave of her manicured hands.

Angled brim snaps our attention. The detective listens
as if to Hermaphrodite half in shadow; half in light.
His eyes penetrate the hazy bitterness, cognac and whiskey neat.

He rattles his whiskey and ice.
If only her skin were to flame
and her pulse to fall and rise again.

The most beautiful woman in the room nailed to a wall

Men's spent voices oscillate room to room.
In her house.

Hud

If a starched white shirt clings to his broad wet chest
and deer and antelope play,
it must be Texas.
Dust, highways and diners serving
very bad coffee.

Look at those teasing eyes.
Smell the smoke's slow curl
into bright sun,
Can this tale be told today?

Where else can a man be a jerk
and still make a woman's heart ache?

We want more.
More of his cool, patrician inspection
of the very core of our lusting selves.

Oh for a day to be Patricia Neal
warming up her whiskey voice
just so she can tell Paul Newman
where to go and how fast to get there.

Just watch the sun fall behind the horizon
casting out the will of God and urging the rise
of demons: drugs, dollars,

the fleeting power of men in uniform
come to kick ass,
and drag the beautiful, the mild, the musical
across piney wood floors
of tract houses and suburban drawl.

The South on the verge of existentialism.
With evil enough to require regret and redemption.
God in a thousand carry-ons
In film reels to come.

For now the jerk stands bare chested
literate, tasty.
Shading those teasing eyes.

April 1994: Two Deaths, Two Wakes, Two Open Caskets: Ron Vawter

I would have had quite a time reviewing your wake.
It was entertaining, dramatically planned.
Flowers, white flowers in vases, pots, everywhere the eye could rest—
the anteroom perfumed by blooming whiteness.
Flowers for a man full of mad love for his generation's masculine
        beauty,
militantly muscled then shrunk down slow.
You were laid out in your "Roy Cohen" costume, that jacket's deep
        velvet plushness
contrasting with the stiff whiteness of the satin tufts of the casket's
        lining.
You wore "Roy Cohen" makeup which made you look older,
the age you would have liked to reach.
Had you not had AIDS, had your heart not stopped in a beautiful
        place in Italy.
"Too soon. Too soon."

You knew the seriousness of The Joke.
Pratfalls, you could do.
But what was better was the right gesture
the swinging penis dance in Frank Dell;
that loopy voice in Three Sisters;
the prim and proper lecturer in Route 1 and 9.
Who could fault such fault-free performances?
Critics and enemies alike enjoyed your quest
for that moment when the joke worked,
the gesture transformed the actor.
The audience let go of theory.
And swooned or laughed.

In one of the miserable years I lived in Boston,
The Wooster Group brought downtown Manhattan to Cambridge.

At the Captain's Bar in a downtown Sheraton, you were outrageously
flirting as you were want to do with all God's creatures.
Your voice a deep, untroubled instrument soaked gently in bourbon
or was it one of those sweet liqueurs that made everyone else's
            tongue shriek.
You dared me to try a dry, dry martini. And of course, I did.
And dare again, you twinkled, try two.
And we talked about what? Poetry, theater, Reagan/Bush, an era of
foul weather and Wall Street Wizards.
You were as handsome as the guy in the IBM print ad,
but then, you were the guy in the IBM print ad.
There was so much laughter.

Friends at the barricades or on bar stools.
Charmed by that twinkle. I wish I could do this memory better.
It was not that long ago.
Not that many days between a winter in Boston (brutal)
and a Spring in Manhattan (lovely, sweet) where one friend's death
left me scattered some what—a story here, a color there.

Greg and you hosting a liquid Christmas party on Bleecker Street.
Somewhat frantic and cheerful as if awash part brandy/part beer.
You dressed like a thirties movie star:
George Brent, you were doing George Brent.
Stylish, suave. Cocktails at the ready,
you were happy with new work.
Pleased to have Gary Indiana set a piece about Roy Cohen for you,
just for you.
You showed us this green velvet tuxedo, a green almost black.
The plush velvet fabric camouflaged the jackets severe tailoring.
A perfect costume. Elegant, yet just the hint of the parvenu,
Roy Cohen on the bias.

There was laughter, an urgent kind of laughter.
Some presentiment—warriors in the desert,
the death of friends. The coarse understanding of death
too soon. Too young. Too soon.

But that laughter, it kept rising near the Christmas tree,
by the refrigerator, just outside the door.
Peace. There was no peace.

For what it's worth, you are the only actor to have made me weep.
It was a moment in *Jack Smith* where Smith pushes back the
        elaborate
fake Arab headgear, mascara smearing so slowly that decade fades
        away,
having exhaled an aria on the greatness of Lola Montes, there was a
        stop
from exhaustion, anger, distraction, what?
Jack Smith's seven veils parted and swayed as if in a silly dream
and you leaned away from us, transfixed by a spotlight
or an insect. How tawdry, Ron,
And oh, so very beautiful.

April 1994: Two Deaths, Two Wakes, Two Open Caskets: Lynda Hull

Last time I saw Lynda she was pleased with the world.
We were gossiping, giggling, giving bad advice
to Michael ever in search of the perfect mate.
"You're looking in all the wrong places," we chorused
as if we could divine for him the perfect man.

As we promenaded the SoHo side streets, Lynda's cane
became a syncopating accessory. Tapping this little dance
of a body in recovery—a year of rehabilitation
after the Chicago taxi avoiding ice, instead hit her.

We are searching for the perfect black silk slip
"to make me decent," said Madam Lynda as we plowed
rows of silken wares in a store on West Broadway.
"Look at these prices!"
"Must be the store where rich guys buy presents
for their mistresses," she stage whispered.

The store manager was not pleased.
We huffily leave.
Start laughing as soon as the heavy glass door closes.

By now we are in full cry, the sun and scent of late autumn air,
electrically charged by the sybaritic
fashions flashing by, Manhattan, weekday
vacating routine, vexing Michael with girl talk.

We find the perfect black silk slip on Thompson Street
A pretty Japanese girl, so quietly chic, we mouth "princess"
is helpful, disinterested, typically shop girl discrete.
The perfect black silk slip will slide beneath
Lynda's black beaded dress, made early in this century.
Each bead separate, sparkling hand sewn by women

in ateliers of Paris, London, Warsaw, Prague.
Women who looked like her grandmother, aunt, cousin.
Gypsy women, runaways with a keen knowledge of needle,
thread, time, ice.

It was ice, a tree, car off course, a tree
that stopped the demons, no stopped the poet,
her fugitive breath. Stopped. End of a bad winter.

The priest's homily is of a Lynda unknown to me.
A Lynda whose faith held her, transfixed in the heavy air
of this thick-walled church. How had this sacred space
become familiar to her? Would her compassion, her courage,
embrace the priest's clumsy sentimentality?
Could the bells ring brighter than the string of pearls
around one of the pallbearers' necks?

Would the lilies trumpet a woman's words as dazzling
as hers spelled out, consonant and vowel on a day perfect
for picnics, lawn mowing, cleaning out the garage?

It seems that death should trouble no more the dead.
But what of a life so carefully packaged?
Which of us knew too much; others knew too little?
No word. No post card. No calls on the phone.
How last days unmasked—her drinking, her rage, trying,
trying to find some way off the chemical battlefield that had become
        her body.
Husband estranged. Best friends tired, perplexed. Vexed.
She seemed vexed beneath the cosmetic blush

the mortician's brush made on her thin, almost child-sized face.
Vexed. Clouds of satiny cloth enfolded her body, too small.

A column of photographs and sprays of flowers situate our sorrowful
walk from back of this square ordinary room to the open casket.

As we pass her casket, we each see:
sweet Lynda, angry Lynda,
Lynda the academician,
Lynda the magician,
sexy Lynda, fucked-up Lynda,
on the road to oblivion Lynda,
Lynda in gentle repose.

Wearing a beaded cap, her mad cap to paradise,
that one way ticket to Palookaville.
Driven through ice, feet on fire.

Femme du monde

Fat, face the color of *blanc* on *blanc*,
smelling of cheap tobacco and many unwashed garments,
from the other end of the car,
the unmistakable melody of *La vie en rose*
scratched against tender ears of Parisian commuters.
"Not *La vie en rose* again", said the young Frenchman facing me.
I understood every word he said.

The old woman singing was no tiny sparrow,
no waif.
Her corpulent canine companion was equally uncouth.
She sang Piaf's signature song with a hostile gusto,
each syllable enunciated loudly.

We sniggered as the singing voice came closer.
So close we began to sing along, conspirators, smiling.
And we welcomed the doleful silence at the song's inevitable end.

I gave her a centime or was it two?
She deserved it.
Was she blind?
Did it matter?

As for me, I am weary of speaking shattered Spanish with
        Argentinean intellectuals
and outmoded American slang with the Moroccan grocer and his
        cousins
on the *Boulevard Saint-Michel* near *rue du Val-de-Grâce*
And I cannot seem to count past the number, sept!
Gloved hands push apart the Metro's doors. It is journey's end.

I try singing Piaf's mysterious refrain, grateful for my own
soulful silly version on the walk towards the *rue Henri-Barbusse*,

a short slice of street named for a revolutionary
or was he a pirate philosopher?

Tired and cheered outside my American language, I am
puzzled with the battered glamour of this city
built for electric illuminations, swift flirtations,
as I follow the paths to dead poets shaped in solemn statuary
harboring the austere lawns of the *Jardin du Luxembourg*.

from PAINKILLER

Painkiller

I can taste the metal
lose my desire for red meat

relax, every muscle
relax
emotion
relax
the time of day
I can give you
the time of day

What I talk about is how
love eludes me
No, what I talk about is
what's wrong with me

No, what I talk about is
what will happen to me

Fear
is the secret.
Always fear.
What you get from me is
the edge of a trace of shadows
and that's all you'll get

I can't give anymore
I don't want to
Everything hurts
This hurtle into living space
and that swift slide out of it.

You want secrets
I say every reckless act

results from a moment of fear.
While compassion is the simple recognition

that what is done cannot be undone,
may not be forgiven.

And a recognition that the murderer and the martyr
the adulterer and the healer can at any moment
change positions, become the other.

It simply depends on how much pain
You need to kill.

What the First Cities Were All About

Cylinder seal/lapis lazuli
Yes, all blue, all the time
beer drinking Mesopotamians
dancing to the music made on the bull-headed lyre

The best in time best in show
best to know that partying is ancient,
inexorable and A LOT OF FUN

But where is that bull-head liar?
With whom is he flirting?
And what is she wearing, breasts perfumed
gleaming curls, black eyes encircled by kohl?

And how did the pig become THE NEW BULL?
Or is he THE NEW DOG, canine, Roman,
that other world, not as old, but just as festive—
togas, pendants, wine and moon madness.

Where is Catullus' napkin?
Was it blue?

Spring Snow

Unlike the young lover in Mishima's *Spring Snow*,
I cannot trust your mouth's promised sweetness.
First love was long ago

On Brooklyn streets,
Cherry, apple, and pear blossoms
Quiver in harsh wind

Darkness comes quickly as does snow unexpected
Heart's anger glistens, all roads are hazardous,
but take them, we must

All Saints' Day, 2001

The floating lights of the emergency vehicles circle wind.
We walk immune to Sirens shrieking.
What if the circling lights were pink or yellow, not blue and white?
Who is the Saint of fog?

Who is the Saint of
our city decelerated in thick humidity, intemperate heat?

Who is the Saint of
smiling eyed pretty girls wearing tiny heeled shoes and short skirts
prowling loud pubs on 2nd avenue or the gray hooded Black guys
smoking weed, talking trash in the shadows of Grand Central?

Who is the Saint of
the Black woman in the pizza parlor who, after too many noise
          complaints
unheeded, declares I own a 9 millimeter, legal,
if I shoot your dog what are you going to do about it?

Who is the Saint of
the boys in my "hood"
who call each other "son"
peer to peer father to father.
Where's daddy?
Where's mama?
Where's the good old days?

Is this the new catechism
and where is the handsome priest to answer?
By rote: do we sing a possible peace?

Shall we venture into this destroyed world thinking
charm, glee, proverbial opportunity

Shall we gather the names of the lost
then watch them float like feathers on the dirty wind

Shall we gather at the altars of old gods
and whine about our lives

Shall we watch the shadows watch us back

Now that clocks pulse instead of tick
are the streets safer for the wretched, the damned?

In what cinema are the dreams of mass destruction
so dear as ours?

Shimmer

how fire begins is easily explained
that's why people hate science

who wants to know
the precise chemical composition of depression?
Can't there be mysterious forces
and the loss of shimmer?

when stars explode on summer evenings
must we match their bright fury
with the precise velocity of light?

Radio waves are a wonder to behold—
speech pulsing like sex with a new lover
and can't that be enough?

My Movie

Waiting for me at the Grand Central Information kiosk
This is my movie, my instruction. He
slouches like Belmondo in *Breathless*
feline smooth, bear like growling
he has his woman in sight
what else does he need to do?

We ride up the escalator to what used to be
the Pan Am building, he feels me up.
One of us is blushing

Garlic, ginger, cilantro, salt
During lunch, he says
"I love lookin at you"

I drop my fork

Food sits in heaps.

Waiting for the Year of the Horse

a full moon or the shape of its coming

day after my birthday, horse gallops in

the lunar year—no more dragons, are we happy

will there be fire crackers, shouts in the streets, curses

Oh demons be gone!

are you the rider I expected or a messenger with bad news

am I your sanctuary or a difficult harbor to navigate

your hands are large enough to hold many things

and to let them loose

one by one

rose petals

coins

my name in metal

explode

Son Cubano

We are at the genesis of a *bolero*
eyes, lips, thick, kinky dreads
beds, cars, stars

a singer's words curve
through memory and shadow
rhythms stumble and stop,
come again, the night air a willing audience.

men huddle near a long, brass bar rail,
shoes gleaming, lips smiling, eyes lit
as women, young and old, stroll pass them
on their way to the powder room

las mujeres motion a dream of sand and waves
a Cuba that only the restaurant owner
and his waiters may have truly seen, heard.

late winter, rains slicking the streets of lower Manhattan,
Son Cubano's portals reveal a theater of nostalgia,
the scent of Havana scripts so well.

And we play along
mouths flavored with rum, lime, sugar, our tongues playing
the *kisses stolen game* as the song phrases
a fierce sadness promised
in the wake of lust's mercurial ascent

We flee these orchestrated memories
our hands in each other's, our mouths hungry for each other.

Our song is bluer, harsher, North American
the rhythms African, yes, as dearly measured in drama and depth.

Our exile is internal. There is little longing
for the good old days when Havana was a mean place
for dark people, but a real fascination
for these songs and their makers.

Your arms cascade a trumpet solo, the piano's
harmonics thrill my back.
My lips are waiting for yours.

This is our *bolero*
accidental
lovemaking   Friday night   New York City
Everybody's exotic.
Everybody's from the South.

Pump

Somewhere, the devil rallies we shefolk fast before sunrise
and the knives that set quiet in their berths suavely
rise to find chests and stomachs of husbands, lovers.

Raymond Chandler slouches his favorite hat smiling.
He knows a woman's heart, how weather met the rise and fall
of that pump that slurred her vision and ate away at girlish dreams.

Heat and ice. The price of stockings. What turns when the leaves
       die.
Crying and drinking and walking the side streets of exalted cities.
Moon howling is never enough.

Half moon over Harlem, half my heart healing
other half pumping last grasp of anger
a politician's handshake.

Thus, the new century finds bar chatter foolish and men on cell
       phones
making the next date, daring to start anew what has been done
and done to death. Sweet talk storm wisdom flung on the floor

like expensive lingerie.

Trabajan la sal y el azucar / Construyendo una torre blanca?

—Pablo Neruda

1.

Do salt and sugar work to build a white tower?
No, they do not speak to each other.

Salt and pepper are masons
building
the perfect blank
a beautiful stark

White on white walls thick—whole cities surrounded with
lustrous black roadways—jeweled paths daunt

It is curiosity Señor Neruda that forms the white foundations
that rise platform after platform floor by floor into air—

Tower as look out.
What is seen—the enemy approaching? Or

Lot's wife dissolving—myth and punishment
elevator and aperture—the eye apparent.

But where are their tools?   put aside for dazzle

2.

Sugar tastes like sex, surprise
Salt and pepper become sun and water or lobby and floor.

Oh these white towers spiced with story, precarious
platform after platform, floor by floor falling into ruin, reverie—
blanco, *negro*, mustard, sienna, and beryl.

Failed Ghazal

My Brooklyn living room smells like roses and ginger—summer
       gardens and Chinese takeout
1975 San Francisco's Chinatown ginger cookies thin and spicy my
       tongue snapped sweat

That taste. I searched New York's Mott and Mulberry streets in vain
       for the same sweet heat.
Nostalgia and fear catches my throat. November.
Two hundred broken and drowned bodies in the Atlantic Ocean,

Arkansas heroine, Daisy L. Bates gone finally, one tiny paragraph in
       People Magazine
and so too, my good friend Peter Dee. Suddenly

I can see the morning glories encircling the window of his
       apartment in the West 80's.
Framing a room where a man a bed a typewriter performed a
       constant, caffeinated dance.

He sculpted poems and plays where his characters, many of them
       children took chances large and small to find ways to be
       tender, loving, despite abandonment, despair, the world, the
       world, the world.

Singing voice on answering machine, demanding notes to come for
       tea, and at Christmas
those loud and splashy decorations in an apartment shoebox size,
       but what a big, big shoe.

Sam Cooke is singing *Little Red Rooster* and the organ sways an
       ocean of comment
I can hear Peter say something smart or foolish and play again his
       heart's own way.

Childlike was he alive in the moment prepared to grow within the
        spirit
that gives breath its business and blood its dance

And we are drinking margaritas—his really big and mine girl size,
        just right. We are
celebrating successes small, private, hard won. I want to cry. Having
        once seen his skinny legs in hospital.

Naked. I had never seen him naked and there he was sick in
        hospital.
And everyone on the ward loved him. His anecdotes, his silly jokes
        echoed across the big Veterans Administration ward

down the hall, into the nurses lounge. His smile would not go away.
He knew that whatever happened, he was alive in each moment, and
        that

the people he loved would be okay. We will find our paths to mercy,
to those morning glories-semaphores of grace.

In memory of Peter Dee

Notes for the Poem, "Beloved Of God"/
A Memory of David Earl Jackson

At David Jackson's birthday party, the DJ played funk songs and
         early disco,
as we stylish and sweating swayed our hips and shrieked the end of
         winter air.

Crossing the half century—who is still here and who has gone—drugs,
AIDS, congenital heart failure, cancer, gunshot wounds

Wine dropped on the floor in remembrance.
As we stepped towards the uncertain future of gracefully aging
or going out raging like rivers in Canada.

Amadou Diallo will never have to worry about gray hair
or creaky knees, his children's tantrums or the daily rituals of
teeth cleaning or praises to Allah.

His is a life forever fixed by 19 bullets bursting toxins
and shutting forever down his heart, his lungs, his spleen, his brain.

Eyes shut, limbs limp, lying in his essence flowing out
towards the lit stage set that has become the vestibule of his last
         home in

America. Where every other Black man seems to be a suspect
as he walks wearily from subway stop to home front at least in New
         York City.
I now know why I have always respected aging Black men.
To have defied the bullets ever ready to find their targets,
these are men of immeasurable *luck*. The sixty-something gentleman
on the 4 train, Friday morning, his voice still Georgia rich, schooling
a younger Black man. His voice rising in anger even as his suit and
suave chapeau bespeaks a man of some power—lawyer, business
         executive.

"They don't want you to live." And everyone knows who "they" are
     in his lexicon.

Here we are at the start of a new century, in the Year of the Dragon,
and we look back to a tangled history of blood desires and blood
          letting
or denial and lies. The violent consequences of white supremacy—
          four young men
raised in fear and marked by badge and gun with the chance to

lose sight of mission and common sense in the shadows of a doorway
where every boogeyman story crystallizes in the body, mind and
          heart of a
young African man doing nothing in particular.

They have an acquittal that is not worth the paper it's written on
and the loyalty of their brothers in arms. But who cares. They
          murdered.
They know it. And, so do we. What are we are to make of it?

How are we to school ourselves? Fight the power. Carry wallets.
March, riot, boycott, scream?

We live. We do not become so foolish that we think we cannot
          change the world.
We remain as open to new ideas and as defiant of old expectations
          as that aging man,
still angry and still working to make a difference that I heard on the
          No. 4.

Savoring the beauty of noise, gossip, anxiety and joy,
We pour libations and we remember who has been sacrificed and why.
We celebrate a half century of moving on *terra ferma*,
dancing away from the bullets.

                    In memory of David Earl Jackson

How He Knows Me

How he knows me
comforts me

It's that we were lovers once thing
It's that we may be lovers again thing

Or simply we love

How he knows me
panics me

Stops me from trusting my own story

How she risked much
Lost a little
Got some things
back

Where I watch my tongue
is how I hear new birds

They are louder
their music stubborn

like believing in the end of things
When we are breathing.

Aubade

Your right hand is infant like—balled fist
holding heart's sound

Last night's drink stole your tongue's usual ease
And yet you brought a storm moving faster, harder
inside me, and yes again, my heart was taken.

I watch you wake and move away
not even tears this time.

A mockingbird makes his presence known
across Brooklyn's backyards

Your hands open and stroke my torso
Your mouth found mine at midnight

Now your mouth is dry from all that tasting, all that wine.
This morning both our faces rough from poor sleeping.
This is the slow unraveling, the backslide we knew could happen.

Your face has quieted, the boy more present than the man,
and my heartache diminishes, more woman than the girl.
Fooling around in the dark, ours is a music of mutual solos.
By dawn's light we begin again to practice wisdom.
My neighbor's radio screams bad news.

You leave.
I go to work.

Blue Saturday

1.

This is that cold spring we did not desire.
This is that cold spring of leaves a green too delicate to describe.
This is that cold spring that will summer heat welcome

Where's my Valium,
my Percodan
my Opium
My lover's mouth and who is he kissing?

2.

He's in Seattle, San Francisco, Milwaukee, Syracuse,
He's far from the blues
In Kalamazoo ordering room service contemplating his next move
In Chicago dodging the moon, the stars keeping his eyes on the
        road
He's on video, radio, in the air
He's in my hair.

3.

See how swimmers return to the same lane
Winners in the water, but on land
Awkward, uncouth.

A woman's deep voice roils chlorinated water—that's what loss
can do-turn soprano into baritone; brown eyes to blue

A country tune circa 1972—is this me?

4.

The actress is blonde and skinny and actually sweet
Waiting her turn in the bathroom line, we talk
Chekhov, the Wooster Group and pray there's toilet paper
How passion divides is central to the plot, any plot
worth its time in our hands—read, seen, sung.

Swung from laughter to tears, in art, is not so easy to do.
All that sentiment, those tears, clever quips to disguise
this ordinary sadness. Lorenz Hart, I thank you.

With thanks to Maria Bello, the "actress"

A Lost Key

The 11th Street wall of St. Vincent's Hospital is covered in *Have you*
       seen?
Photoshop portraits and bios carefully typed or scrawled quickly
Have you seen?
Notations from the living, the loving, the despairing
Have you seen?

The Book of the Dead is wide open:
"loves music, loves fashion, loves sports—hockey, tennis, the Knicks!
loves to help others, loves his (her) job,
loves me, loves me, loved me"

Roses candles heartfelt messages
All across downtown Manhattan modest memorials bloom

In front of churches, fire houses, at Grand Central, police stations,
       on fences —the *Misericordia* of modern life—how different
       from the harsh calculus of private hatred
and military precision made manifest on a September day of
       startling beauty

Skyline reshaped, lives lost in seconds.   In
seconds.

Left behind are stacks of books, bracelets, coffee cups, socks,
shoes dusted white—ghost commerce.
And this token of what may have been a comfortable life.
dropped in haste, tossed into ashy air?

My Angel #1

My angel refuses to be like the others
He removed his wings and is not on television

He's a "he" which I find ironic
But then, to be spiritual in an age of religious
fundamentalism is to be ironical

My angel leaves spider webs undisturbed.
He traces tears and claims salt from the sweat of pyramid builders
He has a droll sense of humor—he's my angel.

I often think that if he were human, I'd marry him.
But his immortality keeps us apart. It's such an old story.

As for now, I am grateful for his ability
to capture curses before they make their way
towards my soul.

My Angel #2

Sings with me in the shower. Our duets are pretty crazy.
I still sing alto, but I want to sing soprano. I want to carry melody

My angel laughs at my desire and allows me the occasional
Cracked note.

My angel walks with me in the Brooklyn Botanic Garden.
He is fond of the blue bell's scent and shares my love of bamboo's
suavity. We listen to the stone coyotes that guard the Inari Shrine.
My angel is respectful of angels of all faiths.

When the first daffodils opened in March 1993, my angel let me walk
the four blocks from my apartment to Daffodil Hill, welcoming me
        back
to wholeness. All that yellow and the cool Spring air.

Bold or bossy or quietly shining, my angel wears his welcome.
Humming, you need protection. You need righteous air.

After Nina Zivancevic

Last Day of Passover, April 2006

It is one of those soft days, girls are snapping gum
And flinging their scent—
Boys look their way defiant interested and if you see them at a
        certain angle terrified.

Oh New York City, eternal dramas of teenagers in love lust mad
Money in this whirl

And their Mamas and Papis tired. Long days at the MTA the office
        the factory
That will close sometime next year globalization builds up one set of
        poor people
Tears down another.

And why am I listening to Milton Nascimento unfolding a silk curtain
of sounds Brazil, the late 1970s the world dreams a freedom
for Africans in the New World,
north and south and Milton is one
to sing those dreams to me. Oh Saxophone. Oh Trumpets.
Oh rhythms Southern African Indian the New World honored.
Oh first kisses and last goodbyes.

I pray for friends in grief, their Mamas and Papis sick and dying.
I pray for my own heart stunned too often by love's promise, then
Left to heal somehow.
I pray for you now gone, more than a year.
Many days and nights long ago, we parted
Our New Orleans washed away
Washed away.

Someone some where burn some sage for me
Drums liberate senses remember
Remember

Spring is the season that demands an abandonment of innocence;
Demands we tease out sadness from our petty hormonal clowning

Demand we walk among the ghosts our hopes
Calling fierce names, soft names, loved names, lost names

In language as liquid as Portuguese or as supple as English.

In memory of Ahmos Zu-Bolton

from REPUESTAS

Hay algo mas triste en el mundo, que un tren immovil en la lluvia

What is sadder than a train standing in the rain?
Sentiment overflows the tracks shallow rails
rampages the baggage area,
whips the dining car waiter into positions
catalogued in the Kama Sutra.

Oh surely the harvest moon will clarify where the road bends
and birds with vulgar plumage strike elaborate poses;
where uniformed guards walk gingerly from one locked door to the
          other
as if they could offer protection from the witching hours

Propensity to dispense violence: relentless slaps
to faces, arms, chests. Poke in the eye, bite on the thigh,
a pistol's report, that leap from the 30th floor
a dangling man's chair turned over,
this young girl's bleeding hands,
love malformed.

Old love magazines, new drugstore *novelas*, illustrate a language of
          loss.
Boy girl, man woman, mother child, old man his young self, status
          useless.
Pain is pain and trains in rain are sad, Señor Neruda.

Immobile train cannot sing its signal.
Wake the lonesome girl child planning her escape to Paris,
          Manhattan or Timbuktu,
Chase the moon or
Stop the plunge of a murderer's knife nor the care of a suicide's
          ablution.

Impotent, train stutters, forgets pride,
curses rain.

Y cuando se muda el paisaje, son tus manos
or son tus guantes?

And when you change the landscape, is it with your bare hands or
        with gloves?
I change the landscape with gloves on
I hate dirt beneath my fingernails
I like manicures, but that's another poem

Oh yes, the theatricality of scene setting is pleasing
like a rain storm's beating the hard green of magnolia leaves

A tea set from Memphis showing pleasures of the every day
a gingko leaf
Darjeeling tea in a generous cup
or is it Earl Grey
Smoke off the barbecue, a daybed for dreaming

As affection enters, we could make a fond scene
letting the sideshow of sadness move to the Big Tent
where manicured aerialists swing from willow tree to ancient oak
thirsty in blue air, searching for the wisdom of chlorophyll

Yellow leaves, a tea set, sadness in blue air
Oh see what the gloves have thrown against the wall

*Murieron tal vez de verguenza estos trens que se
extravieron?*

Perhaps they died of shame those trains that lost their way?
That would be much too easy, *Maestro*,
didn't you hear?
They were driven, then dropped
into the sea, where they mingle with sad ships,
once huge with cargos

men, women, children lost there—the Middle Passage,
piracy, stupidity, greed—fates' ugly hands
awaiting discovery.

On land they remain mythic womb factories   Coffins

At peace, trains sing no more midnight rambles
Or announce deaths possible destination,
as sunlight tracks and timetables mingled

But in ocean, they are comic, odd—windows open to sea grasses,
coral, schools of fish—paying them no never mind.

from SWIMMING TO AMERICA

Beuys and the Blonde

1.

On a park bench, Marilyn reads a copy of *The New York Times*,
Her fellow bench-sitters nonchalant—the staged quality realized.
Josef looms over the ruins of a German vision of history.
He's happy with the ruins.

Enough of bad business.
Now for new utopias.

Who should believe in utopias after the murder of so many?
Darkroom images, a twentieth-century revivification.

2.

Blacklisted progressives whine in their beers
But go on to cheer their angular Arthur
Wedded to the Real Blonde with Reel Talent

And so much pain. How should we ponder the soft fluttering
Cotton print dress enfolding the body of this beautiful woman?

Circa 1959,
Black and white image archived and sold.

3.

When the artist doffs his heavy hat, then wraps his body in fur and fat,
Is it enough to conjure wolves in the last days of an angry
       millennium?

And those ruins: beams, branches, stones carved or found.
Spat upon.

The true cross broken into diamonds, oil, nuclear energy,
A forest of smokestacks scattered like Lucifer's light across the globe.

4.

In dream New York, Josef the carver and Marilyn the figurine
Trade fours—artist and performer,
Gruff beard and wispy voice,
The way trumpets, saxophones, bass and drums,
Pianos too, usedta do

On 52nd Street
When 52nd Street hailed music snappy as a gray fedora
Or vulgar as the junkie's smooth spoon.

Swimming to America

Okay, they cut my lines. I don't have to eat bugs or seek out prostitutes for research. I am in it for the money, if there's money. And fame, if there's fame. And anyway everyone dives into the pools there—babies, old people, men who look like lean fish. When I arrive on shore, the palm trees will greet me. So will the police. I will speak Spanish. I want asylum. Sympathy. The raspiness of Republicans talking liberty. Liberty. Have you been in Liberty City? Do you want to go there, anytime soon? But back in Vegas, they are sharking my assets and crawling across my dreams. Sleep in daylight and you have bad dreams. On the other hand, everyone says my hats are gorgeous, my cheeks of tan, beautiful. That I have arrived just in time for jubilation. And the man who looks like lean fish is staring at me up and down the aisles of the super discount store.

A Tale of Morandi

The untold, oft-told story is that Morandi only painted three paintings of objects in his studio. He was morose, depressed, obsessed with procrastination. No, that is the early version. He was not morose or depressed, but obsessed with sunlight, air, the daily stroll. But then he would have to stay inside with the wine bottles or cups and paint them repeatedly. So he hired an assistant. Pierrot. A man whose talents presumed a precise mimicry. Morandi was pleased. Pierrot was pleased. He painted canvas after canvas. He would vary the grays, the blues, but the hues were troubling in their consistency. Occasionally Morandi would point out the need for a different amount of blue here or brown there because on his stroll the sky has changed light or the earth was more or less dusty in the park. Morandi would bring new bottles, but of the same shape. He drank the wine or he did not drink the wine— there are scholarly disputes. What is important to understand is that he liked to draw liquids from the bottles, so whether the wine went down his throat or splashed on the ground, what did it matter—the wine came from these bottles. Pierrot did not drink the wine from these bottles. He supped on potato soup and thick dark bread, but what he dreamed of, as he encountered his masterworks of mimicry, was dining on oyster stew, tender asparagus with a new white wine as crisp as the collar of his lover's finest shirt.

Kara Walker Draws the Blues

There are big lips & fellatio   dat old black & white
Lynch ropes & a music stand   guitar &
Feets do yo stuff   radiating gestures of chalk & dread
One humpback whale's song of dismemberment
Resilience as trace & consequences
Pedestals crumbling   hellhounds round the bend
Yellow gals rolling 'cross the whorehouse floor
A gallery of dead artist bobbleheads mute
Cunnilingus as afterthought   virgin's blood
Sought and sold   Soil dark & dying   Cotton's
Soft center plucked from its cutting bowl

Bloods' drumbeat   Deviators   Jim Crow howling
Make a way   make a way make a way
(Dixieland)

Some joy   banjo guitar "colored" voice
Swamp creatures   divination   cracked shuffle
Mocking the White Man's brand of smoking
Rope

empty.

After *South Pacific*

These songs are anxious for expectations of joy
As if a jungle will break, revealing butterflies
Surrounding their favorite bush.

These songs mingle baritone and soprano—an evening
Enchanted. Our damsel sparkling spunky and damaged.
Race is her poison. His is loneliness. They find
Their corners and listen to worlds crashing.

Mothers hauling daughters from outpost to bush.
Praising the lost hymen. Bartering for marriage.
The virgin's gift a trick.   "hush"
The tenor stumbles from her beauty.
Under weight of rain, how rare it is to see.

The proscenium holds this bare-chested man's anguished song—
Something seasonal, sweet, desire and heat,
Carnage and courage. Valor, danger. Pitiable, warriors' wounds
Open, festering or sutured and cleaned. The nurses crying.
What we hear is the Little Rock lady come to her senses.
What we hear is the Frenchman's survival, the lieutenant's heroism,
Bloody Mary's lost horizons, her daughter done in by death.
Quick, the writer works to get their stories down.

He maps brutality's expanding landscape
Then finds remnants of the butterflies' bush.
He wishes he had left it for others to discover.
We now know why she says "hush."

for Cyrus Cassells

136

Mary J. Blige Sings "No One Will Do"

James Brown's waxed face graces the *New York Post*
Carnival starts in Harlem two months early

All of **Soul Nation** steps to the curb and kicks it
SAY IT LOUD

Oh Verily, his brilliantine hair, tight pants, and tiny dancing feet
       laid out
BEAUTIFULLY—the sullen city unsignified—tears and dancing
Like church, girl, like church

Yes, this Ambassador of Soul has returned his credentials, no regrets
"Godfather"—a misnomer. He was here to represent SOUL NATION
And like Cuba, Soul Nation remains unrecognized.

But folk visit Soul Nation daily crossing the border to that Shining
       party on the hill
where folk are eating fried chicken, drinking 7&7, and smoking
       Kool cigarettes
While disco balls swerve and curve the smoky air like plump
       women having
a really, really good time.

This behavior continues to shock citizens of SOUL LESS NATION
Busy as they are with their markets, markers, and ministers without
       portfolio

They see only the smiling countenances of miserable men and women
Oh so folkloric in fake fur floor length coats, rhinestones and hot
       pants.

SOUL NATION gives up poly rhythms and an occasional orgasmic
       shriek

GET UP OFFA THAT THANG and make yourself feel better
GET UP OFFA THAT THANG and change the shape of weather

Because some times what you're ON ain't NO GOOD, NO WAY
YOU REALLY REALLY GOTTA GET OFFA THAT THANG

De Man, De Woman, Dis Soul less Nation with the odd
White Man in Charge—on a ranch, a barge, fishing—whatever

Violent death follows.
Best to join the Ambassador of Soul, who brought
us the ache and art of Black America, claiming

Patriarchy of funk and feeling **just about as good as you can get**
When you walk a walk so defiant, every one wants to sample your
            will

And this year, Mary J sings about who will do and who won't
We of the folkloric know that only the **hardest working man will do.**

And even in repose, he's working the room,
lit like a saint and made up
Better than any well-off hooker

Hands and feet hidden beneath tufted satin
So we can't see the wings.

A City in Heaven

Soprano's words pearl the soft sheen summer evening.
Off under the undertow, depth-charges blonde the currents.
Everybody everybody dance at least flap wings and sky.
Outer limits slum-dwellers calculate the whisk of broom,
And coins platter the sidewalks all cheap all cheap.
Stranded here like immigrants streets of gold undiscovered.
Black men from Mississippi walk Chicago's byways.
There is heaven somewhere in those pearls around the white
Lady's neck, but on earth the shit fouls the air.
Streets this mean are so conventional, like a gangster's tip
Or the striped bass with pearl onions at the faux elegant restaurant
Where voices ring the Gothic ceiling's cross beams.
Angels flock invisible and useless—their wings solemn,
Their arms open only to air.

Dream Book

Five two two was the number in the book the number in the book
Before the flames took a character's skin. A friend would look
And ponder the corner of Schwab's second floor on Beale where
The books of numbers waited for quick or hesitant purchase. The
One with a rooster or a crow or is that what I remember? These
Pamphlets promised the triumph of twos and threes and fours
For the Hoodoo men and the Hoodoo women up from the Bottom
Where cotton sucked their lungs and broke fingers and skin.
Where every pregnant woman was a dime in the bank and
The men played dreams from the dream book. Quarter Dreams.
Dollar Dreams. Dreams that drugged their souls split open by
A sun so ruthless, it was universally cursed. Pity the true
Natives of this land with African blood coursing their veins.
Cursing the dreamed son—king of labor, picking those dimes
Up one by one.

for Toni Morrison

Borges Dream, 4:35 A.M.

I dreamt Borges lived in Norway.
I know he's from Buenos Aires.
I know he's Argentinean.

But in my dream,
he lives in Norway near a fjord.

He built a library near a fjord.
People come to visit the town.
They come to see the fjord.
They come to visit the library.

When they see the fjord, they gasp.
When they search for the library, they find mist.

Borges is fond of eating ferocious salmon and fierce rice.
Wine is served from heavy pewter pitchers.
If lucky, visitors to the library are
told tales of delicate heroism and gentle ribaldry.

Borges enjoys the green green of short summers.
And the white whites of long winters.
On occasion, books sway to a *bandoneón*'s
pulsations.

At night, all the keys are noisily put away.

for Dale Worsley

from LIVING IN THE LOVE ECONOMY

Living Room

Marilyn Nance's photograph—"Last Shot in Lagos"
One man in military uniform; the other in a long white robe
Plants that I cannot kill from neglect or overwatering
A peacock feather wrapped in gold thread
Shimmering in dust; the CD rack tilting
Pictures of my family framed and scattered amongst
Hardcover books, stacks of magazines and souvenirs
Two new blue candleholders
Which match the blue art deco era vase
Bought on Flatbush in the Black man's antiques Shoppe
Now replaced by SPRINT
The sharp blue light of this cold winter day
The way I think about lovers who made me smile
MILK, the movie not the drink
Guillermo's fan for *Bride of Kong* Sing Along
We unavoidably sang off-key:

Ay, que pasó con ellas?
Que pasó con las novias de King Kong?
Ay King Kong!
Ay King Kong!

Life Lessons

There are many lessons learned in life
But few come from tragedy—I know, I know

What makes you stronger and all that. Rot
I say

You learn more from what makes you laugh
How much pleasure the tongue can bring and where it was placed

The sweet look on your lover's face. Or how loud **P FUNK**
Could be on stage and off *NOT JUST KNEEDEEP*

The towers falling; a man shot in the back
All terrible, but: What can you do about that?

What can you make of a world so wedded to injustice?
How dare you name the oppressor and demand his head,

His badge, his ranch or those secret accounts in the Maldives?
It is not as if the struggle is useless, it is that it continues.

But joy, where is it? What does it look like, smell like—bergamot
Lemons, honey, roses, musk?

To find it, is to explore a path where the stumbles are many
The curses frequent, but the rewards

Love Come and Go (The George Hunt Painting)

Memphis Minnie's gold tooth
Is shining six feet under
Resonating light the way she

Hummed her guitar into legend
There in her store-bought dresses
Cotton or *crêpe de chine*
Wearing pumps with clip-on bows
That pinched her toes in the Delta's heat

Sitting pretty and strumming the glory
Out of that gutbucket set of bulky strings
And a girl's memory of love come and gone

Left behind in a cylinder of echoing sounds
Her voice box shouting the rhythms of want
Potent as gold tooth shining in her grave

February Thaw

Apostles of failed philosophy unite
You have nothing to lose, but elections
And lose you will even if you win

Some form of tapestry, no sophistry
Oh what it is, what is this faith

In a world that was never may exist somewhat
Not even Andy Taylor or Amos 'n' Andy
Or Orphan Annie can organize this bunch

Of suited, coiffed and shiny shoes rebels.
Oh how I love a parade and there is this

Strange one that bands together Maine
And Arizona as the equal halves of the moon
But the sun, what happened, an eclipse?

I don't know what any of this means.
I do care that the end justifies the dishes unwashed
Sons and daughters let loose like feathers from a torn pillow
bills unpaid, cars left outside of town

Pull Up Pants

Sun light lingers past five, past five thirty.
As if night was a new and delicious meal

Soon the white and yellows flowers will push up
Push out in open air screaming spring

And only the grandmothers will wish for winter
Apartments overheated, children indoors, mostly safe
Except the babies grabbed by many hungry fires
that shows up on television news every other week.

The only thing missing is bird song.
Chilly and yet, the harbingers are on the street
Neighbors hanging outside the brownstone
With the huge ankh symbol in the window

My skinny neighbor upbraids me when I joke
about the belt not holding up his pants.
"I ain't no hoodlum" he declares
as he pulls up his pants.
"I got a hernia."

Second Person, Hurting

This is the day you became a cartoon figure
Walk up the stairwell/then race walk to one east
See the sign turn sharp
And BLAM you hit not air
But glass. Very very thick glass

If you're lucky, you don't fall
If you're lucky, you don't see stars
If you're lucky, you stand there
If you're lucky, you don't bleed
If you're lucky, the nice white guy asks
"are you alright?"
If you're lucky, the nice black guy asks
"are you alright?" and he adds
"I've done that twice."

You stand there feeling blank, then foolish
And hurting, you feel your lower lip swelling
You want to cry but you can't
You are there to meet people who may remember you
May hire you, someday soon for a job

You have not been lucky enough to get.

Living in the Love Economy

I watch my daily intake of Cheerios, peanut butter, salad greens
I can do two major job applications per day
I can lick my wounds

I just got the computer part that won't be around a year from now
I found out when I could send in the payment for health insurance

What I can't do is parse the future
Or glow in the dark

Or lick the salt from your back,
But that was a while ago and how sad to want

Your back right now or the back up or an embrace
That lasts longer than it should.

The Love Economy is complicated: affection is scarce
Jealously traded as a penny stock and pleasure calculated
On past accounts, overdue.

(subsequent to Thomas Sayers Ellis)

Grief list of unnamed dead
4:50 A.M. red lights me
Thus:

"and later the Foucault inspired remnants of a
federal bureau the power visible in ink stamp
and laundry allowance"   I write.

laundry allowance
Foucault

Reading Taylor Branch's *Pillar of Fire*—
Murderous White Men

Spat out their snake like tobacco spit
On Blacks—full citizenship and justice cursed
at Country Clubs where southern governors
can't charm their way out of a future they know won't respect them.

Bureaucrats report, record, write file after file.
The power visible.
Shiny brown FBI shoes—oh Zappa.
Federal bureau Foucault inspired.

Armed struggle or nonviolent confrontation
Ideas collide across dining room tables
Early audiotapes
Positioned in the Negro churches
Where the workers (civil, young, enraged)
Sign people up
Eager or weary enough
to go down to
The county courthouse to

Register to Vote

From want of courtesy, these people receive scorn
And a persistent violence naked but for the White ladies
Who might pass the parade of Negro Citizens
demanding their due.

Negro Citizens' monuments are scattered
Across the county
In the pastures
By riverbeds
On the jail cells' floors
Where bodies "showed up"
Or were cut down (swung suicide)

Negro Citizens' voices prayed or sang or damned
Their murderers—smug Whites—to what looked
like the homes of the poorest sharecroppers

(poor poor Whites)

—no doors:

No windows; dirt floors
A stove where no wood
or coal could make the damp go away.

House on the farthest road,
in the deepest wood

Where the devil found the inhabitants
unsuitable for the hottest regions of hell.

Day After May Day

Tomie's Year of the Ox card stands next to Sandra's
peacock feather wrapped in gold thread, nearby a
cerulean blue vase—I think Jody gave me. There
are always gifts in my house. If you live long enough
you forget who gave you what and they do the same.

It's as if all gifts come all at once,
like the way the sun breaks through dark clouds.
You just look up smiling.

Life is full of injustices large and small
but also moments of tenderness and regard

How hard it is to see those moments crystalline.
But who has time when we jump
from one ledge to the other, trying to keep
one jump ahead of personal or national disaster?

But on a chilly May morning, U2 on the CD
I can see the Ox's half-moon horns
the peacock's blue to green
and the cups petal shaped edges

And offer one more prayer to the God of Friendship.

Family Ties

My brother is nervous, my lack of employment
wears on him, my Mama, and my baby sister.
They are nervous. I am nervous too. Day to day

Hour by hour. My heart rate rises. And it keeps raining.
If I could just gain a toehold, shove a door, find
my clichéd Plan B. Oh, but I am my own Plan B

Poetry on scraps of paper. Poetry on the side table.
Poetry is the realm of the possible, where middle-aged
women find love and work and great apartments

or new homes with reasonable mortgages and roofs
that will last another 20 years. I know the bohemian
myth of living hand to mouth in a garret died when

twenty-year-olds in the 80s made more money from art
than their parents made in the suburbs. But here am I
living hand to mouth day by day making my family nervous.

I aspire to a better situation; a different position.
To that day clothed in the possibility of later
as poems rip through much ordinary mutter
and the clutter of paid bills and plans for travel.

When my life is not so fraught and my family
starts to worry about somebody else.

The Fringe of Town

(après Jeanne Larsen)

At the corner Laundromat, a tall light complected woman complains
about the heat—it's not even 70
She tells the Pakistani man to turn on the big fan.
But it blows in dust, he says.
"I don't care", says she

It's not that hot. And I sit somewhere in 7th Century China
with a woman of the court writing a poem about her travels
to the Changning Princess's Floating Wine Cup Pond.
For some reason, I read this as Changing Princess. But, why not?
Was the court woman's journey a swift escape
from the palace heat; her tiresome duties of charm and submission?
Or merely the annual pilgrimage up a mountain
so that her descent would carry the same urgency?

Would that pond please these women bitching about the heat, that
        isn't really here?
They enjoy ordering around the skinny man who runs the
        Laundromat. He's a foil
for their husbands, supervisors, bad news boyfriends, sons-in-law, sons
who roil their lives in small ways and large.

If given the chance, would they dive into the Changing Princess's
        Floating Wine Cup Pond?
Not likely—Scary items to city dwellers:
A lack of chlorine.
The possibility of bugs.
That chaos of parties- –those floating wine cups.

Sometimes it is good to be at the fringe of town
Just this side of the hubbub, gossip, the need to demand
Obeisance from a little man who is making maybe $10 an hour.

Sometimes, the search for the floating wine cup is as much fun
as drinking from it the first time—wine heavy and tart somewhat

To be the Princess who named this pond, well we can make up her
        story.
The pond's name and festive frame that surrounds the Princess's
        retreat.
Was she pretty? Was she smart? Did she catch the Emperor's eye?
Or feel the Emperor's hand brush her neck?
Did she piss off a scholar who could have helped her escape to a
        convent
before the cups took over her mind?

As for me, childless, husbandless, book reading- happy to observe
How these women's shout a weary pride in their daily lives
Mothering so many or burying the poor men who used to hang
the corner of or organizing the fête for Friday after next
As huge washers rinse and spin and dryers remove yet another layer
        of fabric.
I am the woman barely visible, the intellectual, the possible slut.
Not one of us will jump into the floating wine cup pond, but it is
        pleasing
to know that one existed centuries before at a town's fringe.

Those centuries old breezes from China brush my neck
as we stand here folding clean underwear
& worrying about what to make for dinner.

Riffing off of Shangguan Wan'er aka Shangguan Zhaorong's "Twenty-
Five Poems upon Traveling to the Changning Princess's Floating Wine
Cup Pond" in *Willow, Wine, Mirror, Moon: Women's Poems from Tang
China* (BOA Editions) translated by Jeanne Larsen.

King Pleasure Meets the Philosophers (old school)

There I go   There I go
Derrida Derrida

Lacan at the bodega
Getting a lucy.

Heaving garbage down three flights
She recalls reading Hegel
But really wanting to read
Spinoza. That poseur. Oh no,

that was Sartre, one last Calvados
(the bartender had never heard of, alas)

for the boulevard.

for Erica Hunt

Facebook Profile Moment (God) in Chinese

Grace changes her profile from cartoon Grace
to an ideograph, symbols bold, simple
God in Chinese, she says, it was a difficult weekend.

Serenity, power, health –talismans in
Silk
Ivory
Gold

Or wood—the earth claimed
in figures small enough to handle
or throw on the floor.

I have my ceramic frogs,
Sea shells, a broken plaster angel

Each a token of grace
found in places far from home
now they are home

Holding space in August air-expectant
as warriors. Who will they fight?
What harm will not befall me?
God in Chinese on the computer screen
Life in the waiting storm's whirl

(after Grace Wing-Yuan Toy—her ideograph was of Jesus)

Back to School

My neighbors many of them children are biking
up and down the crooked sidewalk

The girls are talking who is going to wear what.
New and very clean sneakers are on every other kid's feet.
Parents are tallying the costs/cutting what they can.

Next day, these children will put on that
cool for school or too cool for school look

The 1950s lives on Macon Street,
Bedford-Stuyvesant, Brooklyn 2009.
Moms, dads, aunts, uncles, cousins
watching these children playing, scheming, grow.

My neighbors say hello,
Good morning. Good evening.
How are you? As you pass by

Morning glories on the fence behind the Tent Meeting House
trumpet the color and tenacity of a people for whom
few jobs, bad luck, bullets are real as real can get

And yet, there's the albino kid playing with the prettiest
girl, her caramel-colored face stern as she sends him and
the other boys off on some mission of her design.

Who will win her heart years from now, when they do the
back in the day moment? What will they say, shy enough
to remember when they all knew each other's secrets.

A vibration hums this short street like blood pulsing through
healthy veins: constant, predictable, mysterious.

Indian Summer

That old buttermilk sky -song I've never heard sung,
but that title sticks to the clouds outside my window
This Year of the Oxen dragging dragging us
Along its steady motion forward

Forward
fear   guesswork   the drift
Of days found with less of this and less of that

How are we to make of our selves
something generous when the sky
looks like buttermilk and the air tastes like silt?

Answers are few these early years of a century
framed in terror and consumption—incineration

(about)

When first I came to New York City, I marveled
At slowness of a junkie's dance and the dis-
regard of passersby. As if that dance was just
one more insult to the senses along with high-piled garbage,
tags of graffiti, and glass broke up-sidewalks patterned.

One more insult to the day job to make up for night's
True Work. Poems or music or paintings or shaky movies
meant for the cognoscenti, whoever that might be.

Four decades later, the sidewalks are cleaner
The sky is just as wide, but clouds thicken
much too early—Indian summer

(a desperate wish).

NEW AND UNCOLLECTED POEMS

Etta James at the Audubon Ballroom

Someone knocks over a chair (drunk one)
Fight ready, but this vivid sound stops
fists—who let them big black birds
In? Again. This night. What

Flight. Fight. Let's try dancing the blues
to SMITHEREENS. Rustle up those moans and sighs
for the good working Henrys of this world

ready ready ready to block & hustle.
Shit and cuss you out, some where back stage—the money scatters.

Your skin beams sweetness while your voice screams
Where's the fucking fun house?
Your chest blossoms possibilities/ hips thick enough to swing
Which way and oh my
There he stands
In suit sharp as steel and shoes patent leather,
squarish frames/that wiseguy demeanor, the tipped chapeau

You've picked up the high heel shoe you *throwed* down
Then repaired your make up for that second set
The one that promises a better crowd.
Another chair tips back as smoke swarms the littered stage
You're too young for this mess and he'll never grow old.

Self-Portrait as Shop Window

On the bus
Thus the passing parade—All Hallows' Eve

Winds swing the hoop skirt beneath the milk maid's dress
Of the little white girl complete with Marie Antoinette
Mole on cheek

While into central Brooklyn, the costumes are home
made—the best a young blood
In Diaper—complete with pins—Oh, P. Funk or Red Hot Chili
        Peppers

Cheekbones apparent & a rivulet of veins
Rhymes with what—plains, gains, claims, trains

Bus stops & the texting children act as sentinels
Letting us off or on as they please

I have often mistaken the mocking bird for an owl
It's a problem I cannot solve. There are other ones, more difficult.

I listen again for the bird's call. It's mocking me. There seem
to be cows in Roethke's poems and birds in mine. Nature is
ever present even unto this great city that grumbles and crumbles
And yet allows the mocking birds song and hummingbird's wings

to flash like a taste of the cosmos. Oh damn the wind and light
or praise the rain and bright desire for different weather. I stand

in front of these beautiful things and curb my appetite for murder.

Self-Portrait as Midnight Storm

Tossing the steel mesh trash cans is so much fun
Not as much as juggling broken umbrellas
Or rocking the yellow taxis or the last of the Lincoln Town Cars
Ferrying passengers drenched and stimulated

The start of a new day and the pitch is black with stimulation
SHIRR SHIRR SHIRR SHIRR   my sheets of rain
SHIRR SHIRR SHIRR

Oh look at the angry boys drunk and holy as they try mimic storm
The really large guy's huge fist hits a bus stop carousel

It pebbles to the sidewalk, hundreds of green nuggets
His holy hand unblemished by blood. Foolish boys

Foolish boys your anger is no storm and your howling
Bears little glamour—the wolves in your throats have long since left
     you

And here in the rain, your pain is small, durable and yet
The pebbles scatter about reminders of uglier private deeds.

As for my winds, my rain my tossing back the moon's soft gleam
Means little to windows stood still storm after storm—centurions

Of design. They raise my ire and lash lash lash I throw against
Glass; the sash a square reflection of domestic armature.

As for the painted wood doors—they are so easily broken.

Sylvia Plath: Three Poems

Last Seen Wearing

1.

She was carrying books on honor, power, and Frost
And a list of necessities: kids' clothes; birthday cards;
Prescriptions to dull the rain in her heart

A letter from her lover spat upon
A letter to her husband bent and tattered

2.

When last seen, she was wearing
a page-boy hairdo, mildly tousled
(She forgot her brush, she forgot hair spray)

Lipstick stolen. Mascara, too.

3.

Her sandals were found in brambles
Her purse in a parking lot

Her grandmother's Victorian brooch intact
Notebook run over/baby pictures scattered.

4.

The death notice was brief:
Left out—eye color, ambition,
Intermittent doubt.

Sylvia Plath, Office Worker

Tiny paper cuts and nasty chatter
Cursing out the girl in the cubicle in front of hers
What is your problem? Existential or dental?

Wingéd seraphs and cuddly cupids sit on cubicle sills
It's enough to make one wish for a morphine drip.

The aging boss with the unruly comb-over
provides a source of inspiration—how brutal her pen late at night.

Pictures of her children smiling, not smiling
and her ex-husband's number on speed dial—where's the child
        support?

A concert date with a fierce and hungry lover, then
back home kiss her brood lightly, close their doors.

Revise that poem from two weeks ago.
Lights out at 2 A.M.

The Talk-Show Producer Keeps Calling

My agent says it would really boost sales.
And also strike a blow for poetry, contemporary poetry.

She never has poets on her show, he says. Occasional prodigies
Who are pretty or diseased—something rare, but unyielding.
Poets who have yet to reach puberty.

You could become an ambassador for the art—your wit
daring, you know, your charms. Use them.

He says, there are ground rules you can demand.
No mention of the children unless necessary—to give you warmth

Nor the English ex-husband, except to show you are so over him.

But am I over him and why would my children be involved?
Damn this constant surveillance of our inner selves

on television. Like Freud said about America, it's not right or it's
    all wrong—to see our inner lives as the stuff of pixels and
    profit. Damn it, our inner lives

Is the stuff of poetry?   Here I am back from
Near death; my face in the tabloids. One or two earlier volumes off
    the backlist

And this new one sprints about like a creature from another cosmos
Galaxies and planets named only by me.
Oh, how to explain such power to a curious and wealthy talk-show
    hostess?

She wants my words to be earnest and healing and hopeful
Not smart-assed, angry and rueful. I'd stamp off the set in a rage

Or would I sit there smiling, calculating the possibility of a reprint of
Crossing the Water, my personal favorite, and maybe they'd forget

A February day, the awful cold, and my nostrils filled with gas.

What Beauty Does

My memory of a perfect scent: pine, sage, and cypress;
My friends' faith in the power of rough and winding paths
to take me up a mountain and bring me back.

Specimens plucked from that mountain's pastures:
Indian paintbrush, sego lily, ordinary wildflowers.

How I got them is a story of friendship and passion
Nancy, now a doctor, once a shy sophomore in college
Her husband Mike, the second, better one, and their obsession
with the Great Outdoors—hence an Idaho address.

Boise's Northend is a throwback to neighborhoods American—nice
        homes
Next to two-story garden apartments down the street from a
        mansion.
Bikes and dogs and hand-pushed lawn mowers.
Where they dwell is a bungalow that spirits Memphis, Tennessee
circa 1971:

The Who blasting off a turntable, marijuana-scented air, boys with
        long hair,
girls wearing their boyfriends' blue jeans, bourbon and acid.
Paperbacks, record albums, text books piled up—azaleas on the
        parkway;
a howl of buzzing bees late spring just before graduation.

Their bungalow has dueling computers and a real backyard.
While Nancy and Mike's boxes are slowly being unpacked,
Their bicycles are carefully racked inside their front door.

Everyone is a thief out West. If you leave your bikes on the porch
They disappear. If you find water, someone else will divert it.
There are those who fight about the wind. Others the sun.

All angling for rights—mineral, water, air—that only comes with
      political power.

Oh, my friends who love to hike, to ski, to bike and me, they love
Are driving me from Boise to Ketchum through mountain and
      valley beauty.

High desert heat is clear, dry and when your body rises out of a
      chilly car,

BLAM.

From there you enter another air conditioning zone:
a general store at the edge of mountain lore.

This place has everything from Bibles to good bourbon.

I almost bought a foot long sausage. I almost bought a gun.
I did buy cowboy postcards, mostly made for fun.
Food and security. Winter just over the ridge, four weeks hence.

I used to watch *Death Valley Days*.
Death was hinted, but not shown—the wagon turned over,
The wagon train a going.

O, those long-suffering white people fearful of Indians and scared of
      bandits,
desperate for shade, for water, for land flowing milk and honey.

Hard-bitten men and sad-eyed women trekking.
How grand those verdant acres were to be.
What they got was land just green enough for wandering herds of
      long-horned beasts
and no where to farm, no where to hide.

Today, the wind machines whip around: BIG ENERGY.

Horses gambol and graze on that patch of land or this keen slope.
No wheat and corn, not even dope grows here.
But silver, gold, treasures unknown lode these mountains
inviting speculation, misery, and bad legislation.

A few miles up from Sun Valley, we enter a trail.
Mike and Nancy smile and cajole.
Straw hat and baseball cap attest to sun's plenty.
Their walking sticks to the rocks' ready
challenge to ankles and limbs.
Our water pouches are overflowing.
What were my friends thinking?

We slip and slide on the side of this mountain and step aside
for the sculpted women in tank tops and biker shorts—trotting as
        fast as
Nancy and Mike's favorite dog
She runs ahead following the blonde beauties until all is shadow.
We greet each glade with glee.

I am the novice hiker. I am afraid of falling into thin air.
One large Black woman with a bum knee. What were they
        thinking?

She will love the smell. Pine, sage, and cypress.
She will love the sound. Wind shakes aspens. Water crinkles rock
She will love the sight. Wildflowers—whites, yellows, purples and
        reds:
Indian paintbrush, sego lily, the wily cinquefoil.

When friends give you what you need, what more can you ask?
Oh the pleasure in a mountain's power to quiet a panicked heart.
The glade refined.
Hawk's home, wolf's dream, bears far away.

Stewards of American beauty—these are the paths my friends make
        in wild places

—the rise and fall of future walks.

I salute their obsession for Idaho's red undulating hills.
Whose mountain ranges east to west like those in the Himalayas

says a guidebook, but ours is a different story—in this young
        mountain,
on these new hills, circumspect is the American West.

Where people steal
a drop of ore,
a native flower,
a piece of splendor
day in and day out.

Fats Domino Sings "I Am Walking to New Orleans"

Remember when the fat man with diamond rings on both hands
Could walk to New Orleans, head high, heart sad
And see heaven's gate on the bridge to Lake Pontchartrain?

The world turned inside out—strange so many had to walk away
from New Orleans. Strange, how they still know this tune.
Shoeless, pitiless, sunlight an enemy.

Oh Fats found alive
His mansion sunk in dirty water; his old song soften

This hunger for a place for poor people to just hang out
Do their jobs, get by, live like the earth was their due

Forsythia burst yellow past Easter, what manner of weather thus
Precipitation masters drainage, locks and dams. The back up is
          backed up

Three years and levees remain unsafe
Four years and the wars go on
Five years and the poppies bloom as never before
Six years and the hole in the ground is filling up

Fatboy Slim Intones "big bright yellow sun"

And the big bright yellow sun drops off the edge of
Marcus Garvey Boulevard, another winter death done.

"Sons" are wearing black hoodies and red face scarves
School day over; work day starting. Hard times in the cornucopia.

Scratch repeat Scratch repeat Scratch repeat Scratch report
The lines of loss strung along Putnam; around the corner from the
        Armory
Scores of bad choices calculating more hard times
Fish smells, fruit stacks, jerk sauce,
a lung full of curry.

What happened under this big bright sun? Who lost the map in this
        mad wind?
Where's the girl with soft voice? Where's her mother?

Where's the pipe drained of all its glamour?

Randy Crawford Sings "Knocking on Heaven's Door"/January 14, 2007

This was the week when the President's "strategy in Iraq"
was less newsworthy than Steven Jobs' iPhone.

Americans at the precipice—Who we gonna call?
Weather bedevils the Northeast—the ever-blooming cherry tree
in full bloom.

Birds that should be somewhere in South Carolina
Sweep past rooftops.

We are treated to scenes of survival; scenes of mischief.
Our Secretary of State taking to task for her willingness

To testify a failed policy. Oh all this sad news.
The man behind the curtain is dead.

These mad plans revolving on a dime's worth of mistrust,
Misinformation, misdirection

Oh where are our wondrous magicians? And their pretty assistants?
Who will lie in the coffin waiting to be cut in half?

Aretha Franklin Sings "What A Friend We Have in Jesus"

Oh glorious
Oh glory   Beneficence

Benny's face
Drawn many times and with such grace—self-
The way artists draw themselves-portrait.

Rules are to be broken, bent notes of a blues man's scale
Her voice torques inconceivable tales.

His brother gone by his on hand
so many years' before.
Benny's lines brother's portrait smudged edges where truth howls

Oh Louisiana. Oh Georgia Clay. Oh Days of Iron
Oh Nights of Smoke and Beer.

Comfort comes with yearning for a friend's
Good talk/ easy walk around the block
Across a boulevard, into church where spirits surround

Stories rung by rung a ladder of terrors and triumphs—Black Peoples'
Lives. Into the South; out of the South, snakes on the road,
fire in their yards. Gunmen loose like small change.

Oh Lord. Oh Yes. Oh songs sung loudly.
Oh Choir, clap hand, keep time.
Succor in the revered one's Benediction

Then out the door they go
Into bright candescence
Or dark indifference.

In memory of Benny Andrews

Kurt Cobain Sings "In the Pines"

All that aching blondness
You think it's easy to be a pretty boy

starving in America. Everybody guessing
what you will do and who will do you
for that extra portion of the American Pie.

Why scream on a girl you could dream on.
When right around the way, the girl you clung to
joined the fray. Those dropping in on the crowd's

rough hands can bruise anybody,
leave you lonesome. Make you make a blues
that everybody calls something else. There's this strange

keening—like an engine of capitalism, all thrum.

You give. You get a mansion with the great room,
a recording studio out back, a wide-screen TV.
With a two-acre backyard where SUVs radiate
damaged America like H-Bomb movies from the fifties
It could happen here. It could.

Patato y Totico Chant "Ya Yo E"

In this short film, a young man in Havana
Carries two buckets of water
Up and down three flights of stairs
Three times each day.

This is not a ritual but his daily ration
If he does not go at a certain time,
He will not bathe
He will not wash his floors
His T shirts will stay musty

His legs are long and his thighs
Are the thick thighs of a young man
Healthy enough to walk up and down
Three flights of stairs carrying two
Large buckets of water.
Three times a day

Of course this an artistic rendering of
The crisis in Cuba—the masses carry their
Water. But then the masses always carry water

In North America they stand
In early daylight outside the Dunkin' Donuts
Their daily ration, talking shit
and praying the *padrone* pays them at day's end.

"Ya Yo E" is a ritual song to demonstrate virility sung by Africans brought as slaves to Cuba.

Niagara Parks Police Chief Doug Kane said the man "voluntarily entered into the water and refused medical assistance at the bottom."

"what the Fates allow"

1.

Sometimes a plunge is a plunge:
depending on time of day, sleeplessness repeated
seeking bottom.

The world is fabric unraveling, thread by thread
and Clotho and her sisters appear to be on strike:

Enough you despoilers of our hearths,
consumers of our children.
disbelievers and betrayers of health.
We won't help you anymore.

So they sit chatting about how the rainbows used to be prettier
And why the old Gods are so useless, nowadays.

And while one man refuses rescue in the North
Another murders kith and kin in the South—Aisa's list.

Waterfalls are fiercer than we imagine
Family bonds weaker than conventions desire

These voluntary moments of desperation
That mayhem on a sunny day in the sunny South
mirror our media's advertisements for "domestic" abuse.
The boyfriend vaguely contrite; the girlfriend, nowhere in sight.
Should she return; should he go to jail?
Duet recorded and soon to be released.

Meanwhile teenage girls are beaten daily
Leading to a brisk business at cosmetic counters

2.

Our continent's resources were so abundant;
many nations thrived even as newly arrived Europeans
sacked temples and released horses, pigs changing
travel, topography, the hunting rights
so carefully negotiated.

Fevers, deaths, the quest for more land, more gold,
an old story made young again in the glass walled
structures of ravenous plutocrats.

How this experiment in democracy became formidable
And was almost lost in the dust and quiver
Of towers dashed, a crisis fraught for the corrupted
pleasure of a Shakespeare Reality show
Hal to Henry –but no Falstaff—leaving us with

This moment of scarcity, anxiety and change
Making some of us giddy and hopeful

No President, no matter his heart's strength and his mind's
Obsidian edge can do what we all must do.

Seek Lachesis' wisdom. Beg the spinner's forgiveness.
Offer up our desire for a world made whole
With threads from a stronger more flexible fabric,

Illuminated, our future shared differently.

Wearing Mr. Song

So what if her voice is just a half beat ahead of the taped
Strings swelling somewhat over the Mall, all these people
All this color, a dash of cold to keep everyone awake

And sing she did wearing a gray chapeau from Mr. Song
How righteous is that? The trim, just so.

How righteous is Aretha early morning, so damn happy.
A President who looks like a skinny version of her brother,
A second cousin, an old boyfriend. The helpful guy at the bank.

How can you thank the Lord better than that preacher from
        California
Who seemed to think he was at some crystal palace, the walls
        cracked
And crumbling under the weight of his bigotry? Truth be told.

She will have none of that. Oh no. She sings "sweet land of liberty."
Voice crackles in places where once it climbed fearless of octaves

It is still her voice. She's still Aretha. This is America.
And things do change. And change can come.

When it needs to.

Dinner with the Ghost of Lorenzo Thomas

He was wearing a dapper suit and midnight blue brocaded tie—no
  stripes on him.
There was a sparkle in his brown eyes/his ghost was most corporeal

You're still curious about the world, I asked.

"Oh yes," said he spying an Obama 2012 poster.

"Brotherman needs to keep smoking!" he opined
The hole in his throat the size of a ballpoint pen.

Reefer, I guessed. "Oh yes", he laughed.

The digits of his spectral hands shook gestures
What do you miss, I asked.

"Skin," he says. "I remember flesh
soft to touch or rough from scabs on shins
falling off bicycles and such. Tough

Life was/is tough. But you," and then his voice
Muffled something meant for me, but

Oh Lorenzo, what did you say to me?

He chuckled, then rhymed

"The world is always spinning round like a broken toy you can't shut
  down."

Light crosses the hole in his throat.
As if its speed has found just the right portal.

"Reefer," he repeats. And we are laughing

I pick up the bill. It costs what it costs.

I pay what I can pay.

What was it he said, and why couldn't I hear it?

Nothing Is Planned

The magnolia pod still pungent, had it stayed on the tree
It would have opened—petals white, fist size vexing
The dark green leaves and their massive weight—the
Birds are thrilled by them and tornadoes seem to leave
Them be

The oaks are huge too and the willows spreading.
Where there were houses, there are trees, bushes, birds
The primeval all due to property taxes unpaid or heirs
Not found. Or the last resident moved to a nearby nursing
Home to die while the city demolishes.

This new parkland scattered between well-tended older
Cottages, new yellow or red brick homes and the occasional shack
A neighborhood helter-skelter, nothing here is really planned,
Unless poverty is planned.

I kept the pod and a friend said are you going to plant it
And I thought, where in Brooklyn could I plant this seed?
I have no yard and even if I did, this magnolia would not
Grow so huge, so looming as the ones in my hometown

A magnolia needs heat and rain and a quality of suffering
That the South has, despite the malls, the squeaky clean cars,
The Protestant churches at every intersection and Bible verses
On the backs of business cards.

Jesus is always watching
watching, watching. Jesus is watching you.

Stroking the Pigeon (after the film *Amour*)

What happens when you lose your taste
For living things-a lover's mouth
The scent of her skin; his dark pubic hair
His hand's distinct wave

How to savor what can no longer
Offer warmth, languor, curses

This we speak of
Again and again
A theme so lacking in originality
And yet

Is not that taste
It's heat, spice or sourness

That shapes such loss.

Is it not that need to stroke a living thing
That returns us to the pain of what

Has moved from breath?

Occasioned by Akilah Oliver

My Facebook Updates: February 24–25, 2010

Conversations, condolences, laughter and remembrances—loss and community come together—and rain, much rain.

2 margaritas, ice cream, tears

My mother turned 92 and she's mad at the rain. I hope to be mad at the rain if I live that long

Look for the shimmer.

And then she sorted up a poem

1.

Rain mad at

Shimmer look for

Margaritas, too many, not enough of

Ice cream, wrong flavor

Condolences fucking why?

Conversations rupture routine

Laughter brings her spirit through

2.

Circumference of mortality   (crying)
Laughter frames the circle   (anecdotes)
Shimmer radiates frame   (silver)
Rain falls rain rain rain

An Arkansas Poet (Dumas, Henry)

Play long play soft
Play long play soft
Play ebony
Play ivory

3.

*Shangguan Wan'er aka Shangguan Zhaorong: Twenty-Five Poems
upon Traveling to the Changning Princess's Floating Wine Cup Pond*

Translator (Larsen, Jeanne)

From #9:

up in the mountain   looking
far in a single
glance   I'm struck
by the long spring's
start   teams of horses
clog the boulevards   the fringe
of town*

An Arkansas Poet (Jones, Patricia Spears)

Sometimes it is good to be at the fringe of town
Just this side of the hubbub, gossip, the need to demand

4.

Across centuries, galaxies, the rains of words
Feather the floating wine cup pond
Awaiting a poet's lithe body ready for the
Cool drunken swim

Play ebony play soft
Play ivory play hard

Rain the words into floating wine cups'
Open mouths

Swim with horses on the boulevards
Up the mountain's shaky roads

5.

What is the color of Paradise? How would we know?
All travelers who go there stay
What need they of this world's glory

But there may be
A possible desire to welcome those who will follow

Play play play ebony
Play soft play long

In the Memory of Akilah Oliver
March 2, 2011

* Poem #9 from *Willow, Wine, Mirror, Moon: Women's Poems from Tang China*, translated by Jeanne Larsen

The Land of Fog and Poetry

"hates California" the melody plots
this recording of an instrumental arrangement
that old Rodgers and Hart song, brassy
luminous rhythms

An arrangement done in the forties
The 1940s. But oh, so modern
This recording as if made the day
Before this day

In the Cloister's herb garden scents compete for
Dominance, but sage wins
And the quince trees are dying one by one
The garden's soil has lost its own dirty mother's milk

Insects, snow, the random droppings of ugly birds
Who knows the brassy band is playing an arrangement
From the 1940s while the quince trees are dying

Have been dying now for years-the fruit fuzzy with
Sad disease. The curving branches darker, brittle looking

A good friend is now in the land of fog and poetry
Side walking with Bob Kaufman, cracked sage of
Fog and poetry. Another California dreaming

Anxious words on a coast where the ocean
Rocks the rocks.

These are the days where shadows would be welcome
But the sun is bright bright bright and even at night
The moon is bountiful as if everything blue

is full.

I've a decade's worth of sadness encircling my heart
But that's easy —it's just the blues. And the blues is always
Bountiful.

But the mound of dirt, the wooden box, the pretty
Coffin. The pallbearers' awkward grace—that's not easy

I'd rather be in the land of fog and poetry
In the land of shadows and mystery

Today a toddler kept sitting down as if
On strike, her mother videoing her every
Chubby step. Her grandmother enabling
The moves. But the girl was not having
It. Step one, step two. Stop. Cajole
Cajole. Step one. Stop, sit. Cajole
Mama films and films as if the iPhone
Is a kind of appendage. And finally
Daughter reaches mama, slobbers on
Phone. One last chance to say no.

Just look at me. Just see me. Now
Hold me. And don't let go.

Notes

Early Poems

"Wearing My Red Silk Chinese Jacket" is tribute to a garment purchased at Knobkerry, Sarah Penn's legendary SoHo boutique that downtown poets, musicians and performers of color patronized in the 1970s. This was first published in *Callaloo* and was one of my first major publications and was reprinted in *Angles of Ascent: A Norton Anthology of Contemporary African American Poetry*, 2013.

"Spanish Lesson" Héctor Lavoe (1946–1993) Puerto Rican vocalist, best known for his work with Willie Colón and The Fania All-Stars. This poem was published in *ALOUD: Voices From The Nuyorican Poets Café* in 1994.

The Weather That Kills

"The Birth of Rhythm and Blues" culminates in 1951, the year of my birth. Bebop and r&b were born in the postwar years. My birth was by caesarean section.

"The Billie Holiday Chronicles" uses Billie Holiday (1915–1959) one of America's most influential and daring singers as a Goddess figure.

"In Like Paradise/Out like the Blues": James Marshall "Jimi" Hendrix (1942 –1970) was a highly stylized American rock guitarist, singer, and songwriter. Rufino Tamayo (1899–1991), originally from Oaxaca, was a significant Mexican painter also known for his murals.

"If I Were Rita Hayworth": Rita Hayworth, born Margarita Carmen Cansino (1918–1987), was an American movie actress and dancer, who grew up in a family of Spanish dancers. She was a major leading lady during the 1940s and 50s. Her third marriage to Prince Aly Khan in 1949 led to a backlash and the loss of her film contract. With the Prince, she had her daughter Yasmin, who now hosts the annual Rita Hayworth Gala for the Alzheimer's Association. Hayworth suffered from Alzheimer's.

"San Francisco, Spring 1986" "Roberto" is the poet Roberto Bedoya.

"Glad All Over" was a pop hit by The Dave Clark Five. The poem takes place in Forrest City, Arkansas. SNCC is the Student Nonviolent Coordinating Committee.

"Thief's Song": President Allende is Salvador Guillermo Allende Gossens whose murder on September 11, 1973, was part of a U.S.-backed coup against the progressive Chilean government elected in 1970. Pablo Neruda was the Communist Party candidate during one of the Presidential elections. The coup led to four decades of dictatorship.

"What the God of Fire Charged Me" riffs a poem by Ana Ilce aka Ana Ilce Gómez, a Nicaraguan poet.

Femme du Monde

"Ghosts" refers to Albert Ayler (1936–1970), an avant-garde jazz saxophonist, singer and composer. One of his most famous recordings is "Ghosts."

"*Comme des Garçons*" is the name of the retail operation for Rei Kawakubo, the Japanese fashion designer. The store depicted in this poem was located in SoHo in the early 1990s. The figure of a cat comes from Garland Jeffreys' song "New York Skyline," from his album *Ghost Writer*.

"Sapphire": Gabriele Münter (1877 –1962) was a German expressionist painter who was at the forefront of Munich avant-garde in the early 20th century. She had a passionate, complicated and long-term affair with Wassily Kandinsky, who remained married. During the Third Reich, she had all of the artwork done by her, Kandinsky, and the other members of *Der Blaue Reiter* transported to her mountain home, where she hid and preserved them. On her eightieth birthday, she gave her entire collection, which consisted of more than 80 oil paintings and 330 drawings, to the Lenbachhaus, a museum in Munich.

"Shack with Vines" and "Why I Left the Country: A Suite" are poems in response to the visual artwork of Beverly Buchanan, Kara Walker, and Faith Ringgold, three of several Black women artists shown in an exhibition at Sweet Briar College in 1996.

"My Matthew Shepard Poem" is from an anthology in tribute to Shepard, a young gay man whose 1998 murder in Laramie, Wyoming, spurred activism to end hate crimes and led eventually to The Matthew Shepard and James Byrd, Jr. Hate Crimes Prevention Act passed on October 22, 2009. The poem was originally published in *Blood & Tears: Poems for Matthew Shepard*, Painted Leaf Press, 1999.

"April 1994: Two Deaths, Two Wakes, Two Open Caskets: Ron Vawter": Vawter (1948–1994) was an American actor and a founding member of the experimental theater company The Wooster Group. He also appeared in films such as *Philadelphia* and *The Silence of the Lambs*. His last major performance, *Roy Cohen/Jack Smith*, was of two homosexual men (one closeted, one openly gay) who died of AIDS. He was 45.

"April 1994: Two Deaths, Two Wakes, Two Open Caskets: Lynda Hull": Hull (1954–1994)—poet, style maven—was one of my mentors. She published two collections during her life, including the exquisite *Star Ledger*. David Wojahn edited her *Collected Poems*, published by Graywolf Press in 2006. She was raised in Newark, and her funeral in a downtown Catholic cathedral there brought together new and old friends and her family. The funerals and viewings for Lynda Hull and Ron Vawter took place within a two-week period. I went to both.

"Femme du Monde" is a poem occasioned by my first visit to Paris. I was a guest of art historian Joan Simon and her lovely family and was told never to take the RER, the suburban trains, because of recent terrorist bombings. So I never took an express train, but I loved taking the bus.

Painkiller

"What the First Cities Were All About": In 2003, The Metropolitan Museum of Art exhibited "Art of the First Cities: The Third Millennium B.C. from the Mediterranean to the Indus." The exhibition opened a few weeks after the U.S. invasion of Iraq. This massive exhibition presented approximately 400 works including the famous Standard of Ur (2600–2400 B.C.) on loan from The British Museum. Priceless art was looted during the invasion. The exhibition gave viewers an idea of the kinds of works lost to "the fog of war." The napkin reference is to Poem #12 by Catullus, translated by Charles Martin.

"My Movie," "Waiting for the Year of the Horse," "*Son Cubano*," and "Pump" are from a suite of poems chronicling a post-9/11 love affair. *Son Cubano* is a musical motif in Latin music and the name of a Cuban restaurant. Two of these poems were first published in *Black Renaissance Noir*, edited by Quincy Troupe.

"Failed Ghazal" was originally published in *Crazyhorse* with a different title. It is dedicated to the playwright Peter Dee, a longtime friend who died in October 1999.

"Notes for the Poem, 'Beloved of God'/A Memory of David Earl Jackson": David Earl Jackson was an African-American polymath—writer, producer, curator, party planner, bon vivant and like me grew up in the South with visions of New York City in his head. He died August 2001.

"My Angel #1 and #2 are from a series inspired by the poem "My Angel" by Nina Zivancevic in her collection *Death of New York City*.

"Last Day of Passover, April 2006" is dedicated to the African-American poet and educator Ahmos Zu-Bolton as is "Encounter and Farewell" from *The Weather That Kills*. Brazilian musician Milton Nascimento's *Encontros e despedidas* (*Encounters and Farewells*) weaves through both poems, decades apart.

Repuestas

Repuestas are poems in answer to the questions from *Preguntas* by Pablo Neruda. Two of the poems are included in *Painkiller*. Two of the poems were first published in *nocturnes 3: (re) view of the literary arts*, edited and published by Giovanni Singleton.

Swimming to America

The chapbook was commissioned by Janet Kaplan to inaugurate her publication series for Red Glass Books.

Living in the Love Economy

The poems were written during the first year of the Great Recession, 2009.

"Love Come & Go (The George Hunt Painting)" is the name of a painting by Hunt, a highly regarded African-American painter from Memphis, Tennessee. Memphis Minnie is a legendary blues singer and guitarist.

"(subsequent to Thomas Sayers Ellis)" is a meditation on many conversations with Thomas Sayers Ellis about racism, the civil rights movement, violent White resistance to change. *Parting the Waters: America in the King Years, 1954–63* by Taylor Branch factors in this poem and other works.

New and Uncollected Poems

"Etta James at the Audubon Ballroom" is completely invented—do not know if she ever played there or if Malcolm X saw her perform (but that is likely).

"Sylvia Plath: Three Poems" started with a call by *Court Green*. One poem became three and the additional two were taken by Honoree Jeffers when she guest edited *PMS: poemmemoirstory*.

"What Beauty Does" is one of the few poems that deal with landscape.

A series of poems written during the Bush Administration and the height of the Iraq War are included—they combine singers and their songs. Fats Domino, Fatboy Slim, Randy Crawford, Aretha Franklin, Kurt Cobain are included here, as are Patato & Totico, Afro-Cuban musicians.

"'what the Fates allow'" is in *Starting Over: Poems for Obama's First 100 Days*, edited by Arielle Greenberg and Rachel Zucker. My poem was Day #54.

"Wearing Mr. Song" is a tribute poem to Aretha Franklin's hat designed by Luke Song and is in *Think: Poems for Aretha Franklin's Inauguration Day Hat*.

"Dinner with the Ghost of Lorenzo Thomas" is based on a dream. Poet Lorenzo Thomas (1944–2005) was a mentor and friend.

"Occasioned by Akilah Oliver" is a meditation on the untimely death of Akilah Oliver in 2010. It includes quotes from Henry Dumas's poem "Play Ebony/Play Ivory."

"The Land of Fog and Poetry" was the first full-length poem written after the death of my mother in 2013. I thank Zack Rogow, poetry editor of *Catamaran Literary Reader* for publishing it.

Acknowledgments

Continued from copyright page: "Hope, Arkansas, 1970," "Ghosts," "*Comme des Garçons,*" "Sapphire," "Shack with Vines," "Why I Left the Country: A Suite: The Suburban Dream, A Gallant History, The City Proper," "The Village Sparkles," "*Saltimbanque,*" "All Saints' Day," "My Matthew Shepard Poem," "*Laura,*" "*Hud,*" "April 1994: Two Deaths, Two Wakes, Two Open Caskets: Ron Vawter," "April 1994: Two Deaths, Two Wakes, Two Open Caskets: Lynda Hull," and "*Femme du monde*" reprinted with permission from *Femme du Monde* (Tia Chucha Press, 2006). Copyright © 2006 Patricia Spears Jones.

"Painkiller," "What the First Cities Were All About," "Spring Snow," "All Saints' Day, 2001," "Shimmer," "My Movie," "Waiting for the Year of the Horse," "*Son Cubano,*" "Pump," "*Trabajan la sal y azucar / Construyendo una torre blanca?,*" "Failed Ghazal," "Notes for the Poem, 'Beloved of God'/A Memory of David Earl Jackson," "How He Knows Me," "Aubade," "Blue Saturday," "A Lost Key," "My Angel #1," "My Angel #2," and "Last Day of Passover, April 2006" reprinted with permission from *Painkiller* (Tia Chucha Press, 2010). Copyright © 2010 Patricia Spears Jones.

Epigram on Dedication Page: excerpt from "The Bard's *Mawwal,*" from *Quartet of Joy: Poems of Muhammad Afifi Matar*, translated from the Arabic by Ferial Ghazoul & John Verlenden, The University of Arkansas Press, 1997.

Four decades of writing means four decades of a lively, helpful community of writers, editors and publishers whose astute criticism or acceptance or rejection of work helps to make any poet stronger and better at her craft and prepared to expand her vision. I must say I am grateful to my community. I thank the magazine and journal editors who have published my work over the years particularly Betsy Sussler and Monica de la Torre at *BOMB Magazine*; Peter Covino at *Barrow Street*; Susan Sherman at *IKON*; Anselm Berrigan at *The Brooklyn Rail* and Quincy Troupe at *Black Renaissance Noir* who have published my work in multiple issues.

I thank Maureen Owen for publishing *Mythologizing Always* for Telephone Books, my first book publication with a cover by Rick Powell. Allan Kornblum, may he rest in peace, for taking *The Weather That Kills* for Coffee House Press (and for Thulani Davis who brought the manuscript to his attention) with a great cover by Willie Birch. Tia Chucha Press rarely publishes two books by its authors but they did so with *Femme du Monde* and *Painkiller*—thanks Luis J. Rodriguez. These collections were beautifully designed by Jane Brunette and featured artwork: Carrie Mae Weems for *Femme* and Carl E. Hazlewood for *Painkiller*. The cover arts for my books are always by contemporary African-American artists.

Janet Kaplan (Red Glass Books), Rachel Levitsky and the Belladonna Collaborative, John Casquarelli and Joey Infante (Overpass Books—Brooklyn's dynamic small press scene is represented in the chapbooks published by them and that I am very proud of. They are included in this publication.

I am grateful for mentors: Lewis Warsh, Maureen Owen, David Rivard, and the late Lynda Hull, Ruth Maleczech and Lorenzo Thomas. And for my crossing the paths of some serious artists and writers—some gone, many very much breathing as of this writing: Ai, Alice Notley, Wesley Brown, Charlotte Carter, Margo Jefferson, Pamela Painter, Joseph Jarman, Carter Burwell, David Murray, Julius Hemphill, Mel Edwards and Jayne Cortez, Ntozake Shange, Lenora Champagne, Jessica Hagedorn, Bob Holman, Sara Miles, Rita Dove, Fay Chiang, John Edward McGrath, Victor Rosa, Galway Kinnell, Brenda Hillman, Julie Patton, Sharon Olds, Cynthia Kraman, Adrienne Rich, June Jordan, Audre Lorde, Charles Bernstein, Major Jackson, Deborah Wood Holton, Erica Hunt, Lynda Hull, Cornelius Eady, Scott Hightower, Kimberly Lyons, Metta Sama, Patricia Monaghan, Elizabeth Cunningham, Janice Lowe, Tim Dlugos, Tony Medina, Ana Mendieta, Cristina Eisenberg, Steve Cannon, Thomas Sayers Ellis, Tomie Arai, Adrienne Weiss, Greg Tate, Gregory Pardlo, Quraysh Ali Lansana, Rhonda Schaller, Elizabeth Alexander, Carolee Schneemann, C. Carr, Sue Heineman, Marilyn Nance, Lee Briccetti, Renato Rosaldo, Janet Goldner and Brenda Conner-Bey.

Work cannot be made without support, so I am grateful for grants from the National Endowment for the Arts and the New York Foundation for the Arts and awards from The Foundation for Contemporary Arts and The Oscar Williams and Gene Derwood Award from the New York Community Trust. Residencies at the Virginia Center for the Creative Arts, The Millay Colony, the Community of Writers at Squaw Valley and Yaddo were extremely helpful in generating and revising this work. The Poetry Project at St. Mark's Church, Poets House, Mabou Mines, Belladonna Collaborative, Bowery Poetry Club, Black Earth Institute and Cave Canem are part of my extended literary and artistic community.

Of this volume, I have been so blessed with encouragement and critical help. I thank Mary Baine Campbell for her thoughtful and bracing introduction; Sandra Payne for her gorgeous cover art. Rachel Eliza Griffiths for making me look mythic; and Mark Doty, Rowan Ricardo Phillips and Jessica Hagedorn for their generous and insightful commentary. I am so pleased that Dennis Maloney reached out to me and accepted the challenge of bringing this work together in one volume. Along with other small press publishers, he is doing the righteous work of making poets work available and on that inevitable shoestring budget. I thank him and his small, dedicated crew for making this all happen.

Patricia Spears Jones grew up in Arkansas and has lived and worked in the artistic and literary communities of New York and Boston for the past four decades. She is author of three collections and four chapbooks and two plays commissioned and produced by Mabou Mines, the acclaimed experimental theater company. The Museum of Modern Art commissioned a poem for the Poetry Suite section of the catalog for *Jacob Lawrence: The Migrations Series*. Poems are anthologized in *Angles of Ascent: A Norton Anthology of Contemporary African American Poetry* (W. W. Norton); *Broken Land: Poems of Brooklyn* (NYU Press) and *The Best American Poetry: 2000* (Scribners), the bilingual anthology *Mujeres a los remos/Women rowing: An Anthology of Contemporary US Women Poets* (El Collegio de Puebla, Mexico) and elsewhere. She is editor of and contributor to *Think: Poems for Aretha Franklin's Inauguration Day Hat* (http://bombsite.powweb.com/?p=2944) and *Ordinary Women: An Anthology of Poetry by New York City Women* and a contributing editor to *BOMB Magazine* and guest editor of *About Place Journal*. She is the recipient of awards from The Foundation of Contemporary Art and The NY Community Trust (The Oscar Williams and Gene Derwood Award), the Goethe Institute for travel, and grants from the NEA and NYFA. She served as a Mentor for Emerge Surface Be, at St. Mark's Poetry Project, where she was a Program Coordinator and is a Senior Fellow at the Black Earth Institute, a progressive think tank. She received her MFA from Vermont College, now known as VCFA. She is a lecturer at LaGuardia Community College. Website: www.psjones.com.